WARHOL

WARHOL

Eric Shanes

STUDIO EDITIONS
LONDON

For Larry Raphael, usually distant but always near

Published by Studio Editions Ltd
Princess House, 50 Eastcastle Street
London W1N 7AP, England

Copyright © 1991 Studio Editions

All Andy Warhol artwork © 1991
The Estate of Andy Warhol / ARS N.Y.

The right of Eric Shanes to be identified as author of this work has been
asserted by him in accordance with the Copyright, Designs and Patents Act,
1988.

ISBN 1 85170 619 4

Printed and bound in Hong Kong

INTRODUCTION

All art ultimately illumines the culture in which it is created, even if that culture usually serves merely as a backdrop to the projection of some more ideal or alternative reality by the artist. But with so-called Pop Art, the backdrop of mass culture became the foreground subject of art itself. By magnifying the tastelessness or kitsch that is an inevitable by-product of mass culture, artists not only ironically drew attention to that debasement of taste but equally stressed their own detachment from it, as though to assert that they themselves are privileged beings who stand outside society and remain untainted by its corruptions. For the most part these artists simply celebrated pop-culture, but one of them – the subject of this book – went much further. Through pioneering a variety of techniques, but principally the visual isolation of imagery, its repetition and similarity to printed images, and the use of garish colour to denote the visual garishness that is often encountered in mass culture, Andy Warhol threw much direct or indirect light upon modern *anomie* or alienated world-weariness, nihilism, materialism, political manipulation, economic exploitation, conspicuous consumption, media hero-worship, and the creation of artificially-induced needs and aspirations. Moreover, in his best paintings and prints he was a very fine creator of images, with a superb colour sense and a brilliant feel for the visual rhythm of a picture resulting from his intense awareness of the pictorial potentialities of abstract forms.

Because it was as a painter and printmaker, as well as an occasional sculptor, that Warhol indubitably made his major contribution to the arts – for if he had created just films, books and *Interview* magazine his fame would have been far more minimal and ephemeral – so this book will concern itself mainly with his activities as a fine artist, the ancillary activities being mentioned merely to illustrate how they determined his development as such.

Warhol's images might initially appear to be rather simple. Because of that very simplicity, however, they enjoy not only a high degree of immediate visual impact but also the rare power of projecting huge implications through the mental associations they set in motion. For example, the visual repetitiousness that Warhol employed within a great many of his images was intended associatively to parallel the vast repetitiousness of images employed in a mass culture in order to sell services and goods (including vehicles of communication such as movies and TV programmes). At the same time, by incorporating into his images the very techniques of mass production that are central to a modern industrial society, Warhol directly mirrored larger cultural uses and abuses and emphasized to the point of absurdity the complete detachment from emotional commitment that he saw everywhere around him. Moreover, as well as relating to the Pop Art movement, which employed imagery derived from popular culture in order to offer a critique of contemporary society, Warhol also carried forward the assaults on art and bourgeois values that the Dadaists had earlier pioneered, so that by manipulating images and the public persona of the artist he threw back in our faces the contradictions and superficialities of contemporary culture and art. And ultimately it is the trenchancy of his cultural critique, as well as the vivaciousness with which he imbued it, that will lend his works their continuing relevance long after the particular objects he represented, such as Campbell's soup-cans and Coca-Cola bottles, have perhaps become technologically outmoded, or the outstanding people he depicted, such as Marilyn Monroe, Elvis Presley and Mao Tse-Tung, have faded into merely the superstars of yesteryear.

Andy Warhol was born Andrew Warhola on 6 August 1928 in Pittsburgh, Pennsylvania, the third son of Ondrej and Julia Warhola. * Both his parents were immigrants from a small Carpatho-Rusyn village in the Prešov region of Slovakia, in what is today the eastern part of Czechoslovakia adjoining the frontiers with Poland and the Soviet Union but which was then part of the Austro-Hungarian Empire. Warhol's father had first emigrated to the United States in 1907; he married Julia Zavacky in 1909 on one of his return trips to Slovakia. In 1912 he re-emigrated to America when threatened with conscription into the Austro-Hungarian army, although it was not until 1921 that Julia was able to join him there.

Although Pittsburgh was and is one of the most dynamic industrial cities in America, the Depression severely affected its economy shortly after Warhol was born, and his father was amongst the many thousands thrown out of work by the slump. But Ondrej Warhola's resourcefulness ensured that his family did not suffer unduly, and in 1932 he regained his old job as a construction worker, although thereafter he led a fairly peripatetic existence following the work wherever it took him across Pennsylvania and the adjacent states. By 1934 his finances had sufficiently recovered to permit him to move his family to a more salubrious part of Pittsburgh, and shortly afterwards his youngest son entered Holmes Elementary School, where his artistic talent soon became apparent. From the age of nine Warhol was encouraged to attend Saturday morning art classes at the Carnegie Institute Museum of Art where his teacher, Joseph Fitzpatrick, later remembered him as the most outstand-

ing of all his pupils. At these classes, as at his regular school, Warhol was exposed to a wide range of artistic styles, as well as provided with an elementary grounding in the history of art. Moreover, the Carnegie Institute classes also furnished him with a glimpse of the high life, for several of his fellow pupils came from very privileged backgrounds and, as one of his movie actresses later learned, they '. . . opened a peephole for [him] to the world of the rich and successful. He never forgot what he saw'.

In 1936 Warhol developed rheumatic fever, which worsened into a mild attack of chorea or St Vitus's dance, and this illness somewhat disrupted his schooling for the next few years, although with no appreciable effects academically. Naturally, the artist's mother made a big fuss of the invalid, and Warhol later remembered with great affection these periods of enforced idleness, which provided opportunities to lie around reading and cutting up comic books, or have his mother read to him and draw him pictures of cats whilst he listened to the radio. Later, in common with millions of other children, Warhol discovered movie glamour magazines (although, unlike most of his contemporaries, he would subsequently make creative use of that discovery), and naturally he became an avid moviegoer too, idolizing movie stars, especially child stars such as Shirley Temple and Elizabeth Taylor.

In September 1941 Warhol entered Schenley High School, Pittsburgh, where his artistic talents were further encouraged. But these years were overshadowed by the increasing illness, and finally the death in May 1942, of Warhol's father who for some years had suffered from jaundice contracted on one of his work trips away from Pittsburgh. His death not only forced the family to rely on its own resources but, understandably, it gave the future painter a fear of death and illness that would ultimately rebound on himself; that fear was further compounded in

---

* Andy Warhol did not abbreviate his surname from Warhola until 1949, but we shall employ the shortened surname hereafter in order to differentiate the painter from his father.

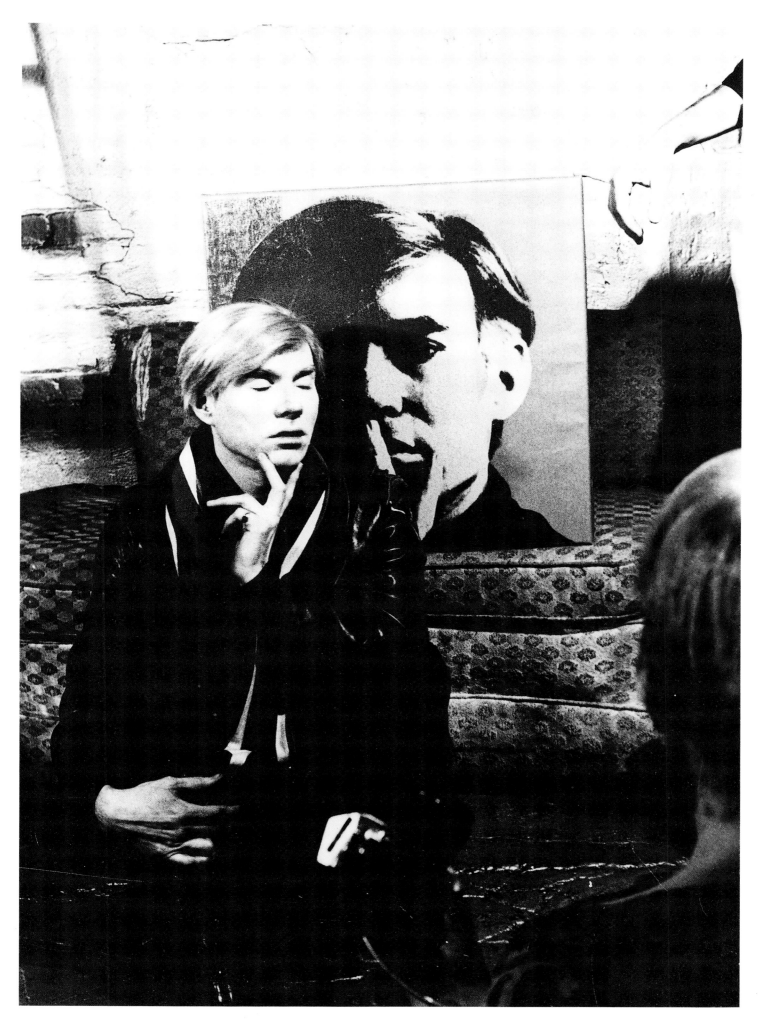

Photo of Andy Warhol in front of his Self Portrait, *1967.*

1945 when Julia Warhola had to have her lower bowel removed due to the onset of cancer. With the death of Warhola senior the second son, John, assumed the role of head of the family, and the paternal loss forged a further close bond between Andy and his mother, a bond that would last almost up to her death.

Warhol graduated from Schenley High School in 1945 and obtained a place at the Carnegie Institute of Technology (now the Carnegie–Mellon University) in Pittsburgh, majoring in Pictorial Design; his most important teachers there were Robert Lepper and Balcomb Greene. Initially Warhol encountered some problems at Carnegie Tech, not least because his thick accent led to difficulties in understanding him. He also suffered from the need to fix his artistic personality; very frequently the timid, malleable boy would produce work that was obviously designed to appeal to his teachers rather than express his own view of things. Consequently, at the end of his first year (and also as a result of the need to make space for returning war veterans who wanted to study art under the G.I. Bill of Rights) Warhol was threatened with exclusion from the course. This had an electrifying effect on him, and during the subsequent vacation he worked exceptionally hard at making drawings of daily life in Pittsburgh whilst going out regularly with his brother Paul on his early-morning fruit and vegetable delivery rounds. By the time college reconvened in the autumn Warhol had an excellent body of work that not only regained him a place on the Pictorial Design course and obtained him a show in the art department but, more importantly, also earned him the Leisser Prize of $50 for the best summer vacation work made by a student. This relatively insignificant award was of inestimable value in boosting Warhol's self-confidence, especially after he had been so frightened by the threat of rejection. To the end of his life Warhol had a fear of failure, and it is easy to pinpoint the youthful event that gave rise to it.

Warhol had an excellently rounded art education at the Carnegie Institute of Technology, for the art department there took its responsibilities particularly seriously and the academic standard was therefore high, with the influence of the German Bauhaus being strongly apparent. This was through the teachings and writings of two Bauhaus members who had emigrated to the United States, Josef Albers and Laszlo Moholy-Nagy. Warhol read Moholy-Nagy's book *Vision in Motion* whilst at Carnegie Tech and later he drew upon it indirectly for some of his imagery, while in another of Moholy's books, *The New Vision*, he may have encountered the notion that mental process was a more important component of the creative act than mere hand execution. Moreover, in *The New Vision* Moholy-Nagy also celebrated the creation of works of art by wholly mechanistic and emotionally detached means, and such recommendations could well have had a subsequent bearing on Warhol's mature practice as an artist.

Another Bauhaus teacher certainly had an immediate effect upon Warhol's stylistic development. This was the Swiss painter Paul Klee, whose *Pedagogical Sketchbook* was also set reading for the students at Carnegie Tech. Yet clearly it was the idiosyncratic inventiveness of Klee's art that most appealed to the young Warhol, rather than Klee's theorizing about the nature of the creative process. Such a visual idiosyncrasy was further boosted by the influence of one of the most highly regarded of American painters and designers, Ben Shahn, who received considerable publicity in the autumn of 1947 when a show of his work was held at the Museum of Modern Art in New York. Shahn's influence became particularly apparent on Warhol when the latter was appointed art editor of an undergraduate literary magazine, *Cano*, during his final year at Carnegie Tech. And many of Warhol's magazine

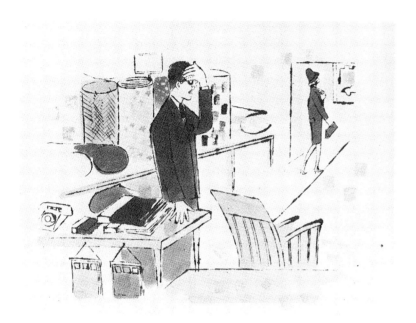

Untitled, *c.1955, Private Collection.*

illustrations throughout the late 1940s and 1950s look stylistically very like drawings by Shahn: although they contain a much greater whimsicality, it was surely from Shahn's broken-line technique that Warhol developed the similar but more vivid blotted-line technique that he used throughout his career as a commercial illustrator. For this process Warhol would make a master drawing, from which he could subsequently take innumerable offset impressions by going over the lines in ink or watercolour and then pressing the wet drawing onto a clean sheet of paper in order to obtain a reversed image from it. Such a technique produced a characterful blotchiness of line caused by the uneven re-inking of the original drawing. It was a method that gave drawings an instantaneous visual quirkiness, as well as providing Warhol with the first of his many means of reproducing images *en masse*.

Other artists whose works Warhol is known to have encountered at Carnegie Tech in the late 1940s were Marcel Duchamp and Salvador Dalí. In time Warhol would actually own objects by Duchamp, and in his cultural attitudes and artistic iconoclasm he certainly would prove himself to be the Frenchman's worthy successor at deflating cultural pretensions and subverting creative expectations. And it was from someone who had actually witnessed one of Salvador Dalí's more infamous assaults upon cosy artistic values that Warhol may have gained something else that he would eventually put to equally good use.

In the spring of 1948 Warhol obtained some professional design practice by working part-time in the art department of the largest store in Pittsburgh. Here his boss, Larry Vollmer, forced him to speed up his work processes, and that greater efficiency would stand the artist in good stead when he later moved to New York. But from Vollmer Warhol also derived another important artistic perspective as well. In 1936 Vollmer had been the window display director at the Bonwit Teller department store in New York when Salvador Dalí had earned nationwide notoriety by pushing a bathtub through the store window after Vollmer had been ordered by his superiors to make changes to the Surrealist painter's highly unusual window display. The fact that even an artist with a worldwide reputation like Salvador Dalí thought it quite acceptable to design shop windows was certainly not lost on Warhol, and nor was the immense value of shock as a means of gaining attention for an artist. Warhol certainly applied that lesson in March 1949 when he submitted a picture entitled *The Broad Gave Me My Face, But I Can Pick My Own Nose* to the open exhibition of the Pittsburgh United Artists group. The selection committee for the show included the famous German caricaturist and political artist George Grosz, but the jury was divided about the merits and propriety of Warhol's picture (although Grosz understandably approved of it) and the work was thus rejected. If Warhol's first assault on art-world values was unsuccessful, in the fullness of time he would certainly make up for that failure.

In June 1949 Warhol graduated from the Carnegie Institute of Technology with a Bachelor of Fine Arts degree, and in the following month he moved to New York, along with his fellow student Philip Pearlstein; both of them had made a short trip to the city the previous September in order to test its artistic waters, and that had decided them to try their luck there upon graduation. On arrival in New York they moved into a slummy apartment on the Lower East Side where they stayed until later in the year, when they moved into a shared apartment on West 21st Street. On his first trip to New York in September 1948, Warhol had made the acquaintance of Tina Fredericks, the art editor of *Glamour* fashion magazine, and now he looked her up again in order to solicit work; she responded by buying one of Warhol's drawings and commissioning a suite of shoe illustrations, shoes being a subject that Warhol would soon make his speciality. When these illustrations appeared in the magazine in September 1949, the 'a' at the end of Warhol's surname was dropped from the credit byline (possibly by accident) and the artist adopted that spelling thereafter.

Warhol was determined to succeed in New York and he haunted the offices of art directors in search of work, even cultivating a down-and-out, 'raggedy Andy' look in order to gain the sympathy of potential clients. One successful commission soon led to another, and within a relatively short time Warhol was in demand for his highly characterful illustrations, both within the Condé Nast organization (to which *Glamour* magazine belonged) and outside it. Warhol was extremely accommodating as far as his employers were concerned, for as he related in 1963:

I was getting paid for it, and did anything they told me to do. If they told me to draw a shoe, I'd do it, and if they told me to correct it I would – I'd do anything they told me to do, correct it and do it right . . . after all that 'correction', those commercial drawings would have feelings, they would have a style. The attitude of those who hired me had feeling or something [near] to it; they knew what they wanted, they insisted; sometimes they got very emotional. The process of doing work in commercial art was machine-like, but the attitude had feeling to it.

Later, as a mature artist, Warhol would react against this imparting of 'feeling' to images made by such an industrialized process, and he would thereby achieve a much greater congruity between cause and effect.

In March 1950 Warhol moved to an apartment on West 103rd Street that he shared with a shifting population of up to 17 other tenants. Here he laboured over his illustrations day and night amid pretty squalid conditions, although later that year his surroundings improved when he took over an apartment on East 24th Street and soon found himself its sole occupant after his flatmate returned to Pittsburgh. Throughout 1950 Warhol's career was on the up and up, and by the following year he was creating his first drawings for television, not only making promotional works for NBC programmes but even for a short while forcing himself to get up at 5 am in order to sketch the necessary patterns on the weather map for the morning news programme. And in September 1951 one of his drawings, reproduced as a full-page advertisement in the *New York Times* to advertise a forthcoming radio crime programme, greatly boosted his professional reputation through its visual impact (two years later the design won him his first Art Directors' Club Gold Medal).

Soon afterwards Warhol moved yet again, to another

slummy apartment located at 216 East 75th Street. There he was joined by his mother who henceforth would live with him continuously almost up until her death some 20 years later. In June 1952 the artist held his first exhibition. This was mounted at the Hugo Gallery on East 55th Street and comprised a suite of 15 drawings based on the writings of Truman Capote. Warhol idolized Capote and he had not been long in New York before he had forced himself on the writer's attention by constantly telephoning or writing to him; eventually Capote gave up trying to ignore the designer. The Capote drawings exhibition gained one or two reviews but Warhol sold nothing. By now, though, his commercial career was constantly gaining pace, and in the spring of 1953 he obtained the services of an agent, Fritzie Miller, who had excellent contacts at up-market magazines such as *Vogue* and *Harper's Bazaar*. Within a short time Warhol had become the most sought-after fashionwear illustrator in New York. He also became very active as a book illustrator, adorning, with Fred McCarroll and Mary Suzuki, *Amy Vanderbilt's Complete Book of Etiquette* and producing privately published books of drawings with whimsical titles such as *A is an Alphabet* and *Love is a Pink Cake*, on which he collaborated with one of his boyfriends, Ralph Ward.

Warhol had first discovered his latent homosexuality when he was still a student in Pittsburgh, but naturally, within such a relatively narrow environment, he had been very guarded about his sexual preferences. In the more tolerant surroundings of New York he felt less inhibited and initially indulged his proclivities to the full, although after the first shock of freedom had worn off he was not particularly promiscuous, and he became even less so as he got older. Indeed, Warhol thereafter formed a number of fairly committed relationships, such as that with Charles Lisanby whom he met in the autumn of 1954,

and to whom he was close for about ten years; in the summer of 1956 the two men even travelled around the world together on vacation. In time Warhol would form other relationships and frequently become infatuated, but for the most part he played down his sexual persona, and often he sublimated his sexuality into a highly manipulative voyeurism.

In 1954 Warhol held three shows of work at the Loft Gallery on East 45th Street, the first of which was slated in the press by the critic and painter Fairfield Porter not because of the images on show but because Warhol had had the temerity to try and straddle the applied and fine art worlds. In this year Warhol also published further books, such as *Twenty-five Cats Name [sic] Sam and One Blue Pussy*, which he retailed (along with his drawings) mainly through the Serendipity general store and restaurant on 58th Street. The books never sold in large numbers but they formed very useful presents to art directors when soliciting work, as did a host of other attractive designs and cards. Such self-promotional ploys often paid off, and by 1954 the designer was so busy that he took on a studio assistant, Vito Giallo, who had previously worked at the Loft Gallery as its assistant director. For a short time Warhol was also instrumental in designing sets and programmes for the *Theater 12* group, and even acted in a couple of their productions, albeit not very well; he did not have the self-confidence to project himself well to an audience, although with some careful coaching he did improve in time. But he appears to have taken a real interest in the theatre, and through his link with the *Theater 12* group he may well have had his attention drawn to Brecht's theories concerning alienation, there certainly being parallels between those theories and aspects of his own mature aesthetic and behaviour.

In 1955 Warhol took his biggest step as an illustrator by

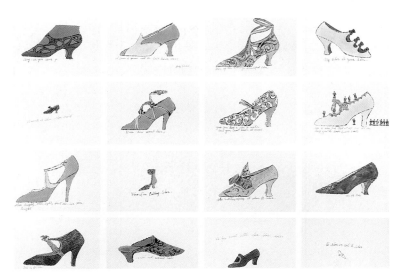

A la Recherche du Shoe Perdu, *1955, The Estate of Andy Warhol.*

obtaining the commission for a series of designs to appear almost weekly in the *New York Times* Sunday editions advertising the highly fashionable I. Miller shoe store. Warhol's shoe illustrations had an enormous impact, and this success contributed to his growing income, which in the following year topped $100,000, a huge sum for one so young. The burdens the demands for work placed upon Warhol led him to replace Vito Giallo in the autumn of 1955 with another studio assistant, Nathan Gluck, who would go on working for him until 1964. Gluck had good contacts in the retail trade: he arranged for Warhol to design window displays for the Bonwit Teller department store (where Warhol had no problems with the management, unlike Salvador Dalí nearly 20 years earlier), and this commission led him to design window displays for other stores such as Tiffany's and I. Miller. Warhol sold many of the original I. Miller shoe advertisement drawings through the Serendipity shop, and subsequently he produced a book of highly whimsical drawings of shoes entitled *A la Recherche du Shoe Perdu*. Shoes were objects to which he was sexually attracted; he collected hundreds

of pairs of them and, athletically, liked to kiss the shod feet of his boyfriends when making love to them. And he was also highly voyeuristic, creating an ongoing series of drawings of sexual organs for a proposed book, as well as a portfolio of studies of beautiful young males and their beribboned private parts which he published under the title of *Drawings for a Boy Book*.

In February 1956 Warhol held an exhibition of the *Boy Book* designs and the book itself at the Bodley Gallery on East 60th Street; he sold only a small number of the drawings, but that April the gallery owner, David Mann, managed to get some of Warhol's latest works into the *Recent Drawings U.S.A.* show at the Museum of Modern Art, New York. In the summer Warhol visited the Far East, India and Europe with Charles Lisanby, a trip that nearly terminated their friendship through the stress it put on it. He also received the 35th annual Art Directors' Club award for his I. Miller shoe advertisements. By now Warhol's success had enabled him to take a second apartment at 242 Lexington Avenue (into which he moved his mother) and to begin his career as a serious collector of works of art and incunabula; his initial purchases included pieces by Picasso, Braque, Klee and Magritte. Eventually Warhol's holdings would become immense and be heightened by his refusal ever to throw anything away, as well as by his proclivity for purchasing in bulk – he could never resist a bargain. (In 1988, after his death, it would take nine days to auction off his collection of thousands of objects in New York.)

Warhol held another exhibition at the Bodley Gallery in December 1956, entitled the *Crazy Golden Slipper or Shoes Shoe in America*. This comprised a series of gilded shoe images, each with the name of some leading media or showbiz personality attached, such as Truman Capote, Mae West and Elvis Presley. Unlike the previous exhibition, the show was a success, and it not only gained the artist sales but also a two-page spread in *Life* magazine in January 1957, although Warhol was not too pleased with the coverage, for it described him merely as being a 'commercial artist' and already he had higher ambitions. Yet for the time being he ploughed on with his highly profitable career as a designer, and later that year he received further recognition by winning an Award for Distinctive Merit from the New York Art Directors' Club for one of his I. Miller shoe advertisements. On the personal front Warhol had an operation to reduce the size of his slightly bulbous nose, but this had little effect, although he did radically improve his appearance from about the same time onwards by covering his rapidly balding pate with wigs.

At the end of 1957 Warhol held yet another exhibition of gilded drawings at the Bodley Gallery, and he published the related *Gold Book* as a Christmas self-promotional item. But just four weeks later, in January 1958, an exhibition opened at the Leo Castelli Gallery in New York that would ultimately change Warhol's entire life. This was the first large-scale showing of Jasper Johns's paintings of the American flag, targets and numbers, and the challenge such images offered to the prevailing aesthetic trend of the day was consolidated a mere two months later by an exhibition (also held at the Castelli Gallery) of works by Robert Rauschenberg. Between them these two artists brought about a radical break with the direction that recent American art had been taking.

Throughout the late 1940s and the 1950s, American artists such as Jackson Pollock, Arshile Gorky, Willem de Kooning, Franz Kline, Clyfford Still, Mark Rothko and Barnett Newman had been giving American art the aesthetic lead over French art by exploring the psychological, expressive or colouristic basics of painterly process in ways that fulfilled the implications of surrealism,

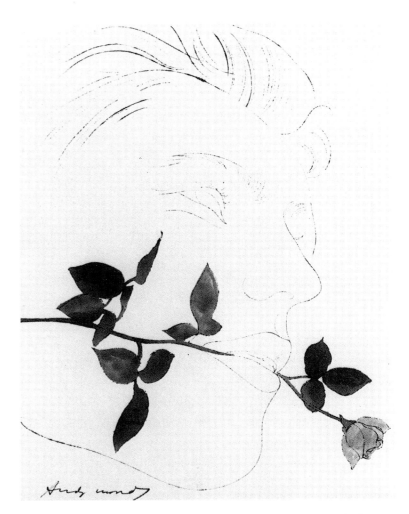

Young man with a flower (*from* A Gold Book by Andy Warhol), *1957, Private Collection.*

expressionism or colour abstraction, whilst usually ditching representationalism altogether. This group of artists, principally based in New York, has frequently been lumped together as constituting a group of 'abstract expressionists' (although de Kooning retained representation in his visual language, and Rothko and Newman were anything but expressionistic artists), but what did link them was their shared determination to create an art touching upon the fundamentals of emotional energy, intellectual seriousness and spiritual value. In the face of

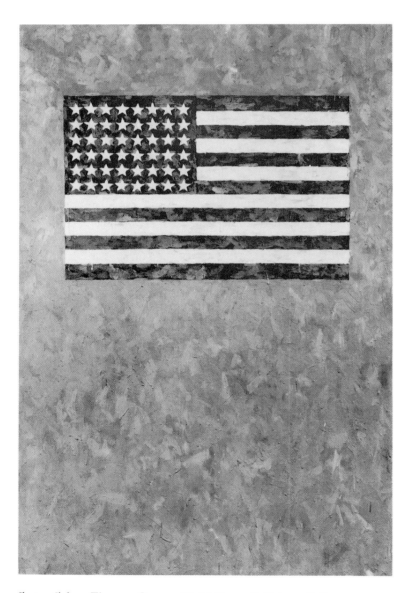

Jasper Johns, Flag on Orange Field II, *1958, Private Collection.*

such elevated aspirations the throwaway, neo-Dada gestures of Johns and Rauschenberg, which also looked to the familiar imagery of contemporary mass culture, seemed wholly subversive. Thus in works like his American flag pictures, Johns redeployed the familiar quasi-expressionistic brushwork of the previous artistic

generation in ways that paradoxically and ironically enjoyed no expressive intention whatsoever; equally he stressed the flag's cultural centrality to America while simultaneously removing it from the symbolic realm altogether through his deadpan treatment of it as an art object. Neither Johns nor Rauschenberg can be considered Pop artists, for they were not primarily interested in the mass culture around them; mostly they were playing games with artistic language and significance, carrying on the kinds of games with meanings and accepted notions of art that had first been developed in Europe in the 1920s, and which Marcel Duchamp had then brought to the United States. But the appropriation by Johns and Rauschenberg of imagery from mass culture rubbed off on Warhol, and, like them, in time he too would call into question the very nature of a work of art itself.

The Johns and Rauschenberg shows of 1958 gave Warhol an intense desire to break with 'commercial' art and instead become a fine artist, although by now his financial commitments were so huge that it took him at least two more years to make that break (and in order to retain a possible means of retreat to his lucrative career as a designer, he went on surreptitiously making commercial designs until 1964 through Nathan Gluck). In 1959 Warhol lost the I. Miller shoe account, due to a company decision to use photographs rather than drawings for the advertisement illustrations, although he still had plenty of other advertising work and received the Certificate of Excellence from the American Institute of Graphic Arts for his previous year's output. By now he had bought a town-house at 1342 Lexington Avenue between 89th and 90th Streets for $67,000, and he moved his mother into its basement, which he fitted out as an apartment for her. That autumn he published a joke cookbook, *Wild Raspberries*, the text for which was provided by Suzie Frankfurt, and he held an exhibition of the drawings made for the book at the Bodley Gallery in December 1959, although by now there was little market for such offerings; New York taste was moving away from Warhol's fey imagery. Faced with this marginalization, and by the growing acclaim accorded to artists such as Johns and Rauschenberg, Warhol felt increasingly desperate about the creative *cul de sac* into which he was heading.

As with the threat of dismissal that had confronted him in his first year at art school some 15 years earlier, the possibility of failure galvanized Warhol into action, and from late 1959 onwards he slaved away at his canvases during his spare time in the hope that something would emerge. In 1960 he even made works in the neo-Dada vein that Rauschenberg was mapping out by urinating on some white canvases as an anti-art gesture (a process he would repeat in the *Oxidation* paintings of the late 1970s) and by placing some blank canvases on the pavement outside the house on Lexington Avenue so that the footmarks left on them by passing pedestrians would constitute a random 'artistic' statement, but he soon realized that such gestures were not leading him anywhere. Instead, he began painting mass-culture objects such as Coca-Cola bottles, food cans, refrigerators and television sets, appropriating his imagery from cheap advertisements and comic strips in works that were inspired in equal parts by Johns's use of newsprint as the support for some of his Flags paintings, by the mixture of a quasi-expressionist brushwork with subject-matter drawn from popular culture in the works of both Johns and Rauschenberg (whose pictures he outwardly derided because he maintained he could do better), and by the emotional detachment that underlay their work. And when Warhol showed two of the resulting efforts to his friend, the film-maker Emile de Antonio, he was left in no doubt that he was on the right track; as the painter later recalled:

After I'd done my first canvases, De [Antonio] was the first person I wanted to show them to. He could always see the value of something right off . . . At five o'clock one particular afternoon the doorbell rang and De came in and sat down. I poured Scotch for us, and then I went over to where two paintings I'd done, each about six feet high and three feet wide, were propped, facing the wall. I turned them around and placed them side by side against the wall and then I backed away to take a look at them myself. One of them was a Coke bottle with Abstract Expressionist hash marks halfway up the side. The second one was just a stark, outlined Coke bottle in black and white. I didn't say a thing to De. I didn't have to – he knew what I wanted to know.

'Well, look, Andy,' he said after staring at them for a couple of minutes. 'One of these is a piece of shit, simply a little bit of everything. The other is remarkable – it's our society, it's who we are, it's absolutely beautiful and naked, and you ought to destroy the first one and show the other.'

That afternoon was an important one for me.

Boosted by such encouragement, Warhol began to put out feelers for a gallery to show his work, although he encountered strong resistance from leading art dealers such as Richard Bellamy, Sidney Janis, Martha Jackson and Robert Elkron, due mainly to his prevailing image as a 'commercial artist'. But one person who did take Warhol seriously was Leo Castelli's assistant, Ivan Karp, and in turn he introduced Warhol to an assistant curator of twentieth-century American art at the Metropolitan Museum of Art, Henry Geldzahler. Karp also tried to get his boss interested in showing Warhol's work but unfortunately Castelli did not at first want to exhibit the pictures. Although Warhol had dropped comic-strip imagery from his paintings when he learned that another

New York artist, Roy Lichtenstein, was also employing such source material, Castelli felt that the imagery of the two painters was too alike; as he already represented Lichtenstein he could not handle Warhol as well. But if prestigious dealers refused to take the painter seriously, nonetheless he had other ways of putting his pictures before the public: in April 1961 he exhibited several of them (including the *Saturday's Popeye* reproduced on page 47) in one of the 57th Street side windows of Bonwit Teller's department store.

By now Warhol's commitment to painting was costing him dear, for he was neglecting his commercial art opportunities; as he subsequently told his brother, his income in 1960 went down to a mere $60,000, which was still a comparatively huge sum but which his lavish lifestyle quickly gobbled up. Faced with these financial problems Warhol began to sell his paintings at knock-down prices to collectors such as Robert Scull, who was supporting the new wave of painters; as Scull later told Emile de Antonio:

I went to see [Warhol] early in 1961, and he said to me, 'I want to sell you some paintings.'
And I said, 'What do you mean, "some" paintings?'
He said, 'Well, I don't care how many you take, but I need $1,400.'
I said, 'What do you think this is?' I couldn't get used to the idea.
He said, 'Look, here are five pictures.'
I was really overwhelmed by the art. The art was sensational.
Then he said to me, 'Well, if that won't do, here's another one. As long as it's $1,400, you can take whatever you want.'
I said, 'You're completely mad,' but my first purchase of Warhol consisted of $1,400 worth of art.

Yet in the final analysis money was not Warhol's most pressing need; he wanted fame, and to achieve that he required an imagery that would force the world to take him seriously as an artist. By the end of 1961 he was no nearer to fulfilling that need than he had been at the onset of his fine-art career, and he was deeply depressed because of it. Throughout the New York art scene a new wave of painters and sculptors was making itself known through its adoption of imagery from mass culture, and Warhol was in danger of getting left behind. But finally the problem resolved itself one evening in December 1961. Warhol got talking to an interior decorator and gallery owner acquaintance, Muriel Latow, and she gave him exactly what he needed, albeit for a price; as a mutual friend, Ted Carey, later related:

... Andy said, 'I've got to do something ... The cartoon paintings ... it's too late. I've got to do something that really will have a lot of impact, that will be different enough from Lichtenstein and Rosenquist, that will be very personal, that won't look like I'm doing *exactly* what they're doing ... I don't know what to do. So, Muriel, you've got fabulous ideas. Can't you give me an idea?' And Muriel said, 'Yes, but it's going to cost you money.' So Andy said, 'How much?' She said, 'Fifty dollars ... get your checkbook and write me a check for fifty dollars.' And Andy ran and got his checkbook, like, you know, he was really crazy and he wrote out the check. He said, 'All right, give me a fabulous idea.' And so Muriel said, 'What do you like more than anything else in the world?' So Andy said, 'I don't know. What?' So she said, 'Money. The thing that means more to you and that you like more than anything else in the world is money. You should paint pictures of money.' And so Andy said, 'Oh, that's wonderful.' 'So then either that or,' she said, 'you've got to find something that's recognizable to almost everybody. Something that you see every day that everybody would recognize. Something like a can of Campbell's soup.' So Andy said, 'Oh, that sounds fabulous.' So, the next day Andy went out to the supermarket (because we all went by the next day), and we came in, and he had a case of . . . all the soups. So that's how [he got] the idea of the *Money* and *Soup* paintings.

This would not be the last time that Warhol would obtain some of his most important ideas from others, as we shall see, but that he received them in this way does not in any way negate the originality of those ideas, for ultimately it was he who carried their visual, aesthetic and cultural potential through to fruition and, in any case they took root in ground that he had been a long time in preparing, as will shortly become clear. Naturally, for anyone who had spent as long as Warhol had done as a commercial artist receiving instructions on the visual direction of his imagery, it was entirely natural to think of the creation of the images as a collaborative effort, and a major virtue of Warhol's gleaning of ideas from others was that the painter served to focus ideas and responses permeating his surrounding culture. Warhol himself was very open about the derivation of his works, for as he stated in *POPism: The Warhol '60s*:

I was never embarrassed about asking someone, literally, 'What should I paint?' because Pop comes from the outside, and how is asking someone for ideas any different from looking for them in a magazine? . . . That kind of thing would go on for weeks whenever I started a new project – asking everyone I was with what they thought I should do. I still do it. That's one thing that has never changed; I hear one word, or maybe misunderstand somebody, and that puts me on to a good idea of my own . . .

Inspired by the ideas he had purchased from Muriel Latow, Warhol immediately set to work painting pictures of both money and of cans of Campbell's soup – the latter objects being equally close to his heart, as he had eaten soup and crackers daily for his lunch for over 20 years. All through the winter and spring of 1962 Warhol worked on pictures of dollars in various combinations, both as individual bills and in rows, and also upon a set of 32 small canvases that each featured one of the 32 different varieties of Campbell's soups on a blank background. And this is where Warhol's conceptual and visual genius took over from Muriel Latow's original idea, for the quality of deadpan statement that the artist accorded to his images enforced a rigid disconnection from emotion, whilst their machine-like appearance exactly reflected the industrial processes that had brought the objects they represented into being in the first place. Warhol was making a comment on the bloodless imagery of the machine age through directly reflecting its mechanistic divorce from emotion in his own imagery. And some remarks that the artist made in 1962 about a picture entitled *Storm Door* (Melzer Collection, USA) that he had painted two years earlier and which shows a sharp-edged image of a glazed door unit with the price attached, demonstrate that he had been wanting to express such a divorce for a fairly long time:

I adore America and these are some comments on it. My image is a statement of the symbols of the harsh, impersonal products and brash materialistic objects on which America is built today. It is a projection of everything that can be bought and sold, the practical but impermanent symbols that sustain us.

Muriel Latow's ideas had therefore taken root in very fertile soil. And for Warhol such imagistic mechanization probably reflected a social mechanization as well; as he told Gene Swenson in 1963:

Someone said Brecht wanted everybody to think alike. I want everybody to think alike . . . Everybody looks alike and acts alike, and we're getting more and more that way. I think everybody should be a machine . . . because you do the same thing every time. You do it again and again . . . History books are being rewritten all the time. It doesn't matter what you do. Everybody just goes on thinking the same thing, and every year it gets more and more alike. Those who talk about individuality the most are the ones who most object to deviation, and in a few years it may be the other way round. Some day everybody will think just what they want to think, and then everybody will probably be thinking alike; that seems to be what is happening.

Naturally, any reasonably intelligent person who had lived through the McCarthyite phase of the Cold War in America would have been well aware of recent pressures towards intellectual conformism, while in the remark about deviation one might even detect a note of protest concerning hypocritical attitudes towards sexual non-conformism. But undoubtedly Warhol was making larger points here about the repetitiousness and conformism that underlie much of modern life generally, just as through repetitiousness and visual patterning his pictures were making exactly those self-same points about the imagery of mass culture and the reality behind it. And from this time onwards Warhol equally began to cultivate a public persona *as* a machine; as he also told Gene Swenson in 1963, 'I think everybody should be a machine . . . I want to be a machine, and I feel that

whatever I do and do machine-like is what I want to do.' Yet he did not want to be a machine just for its own sake; instead, by means of such an affected stance he could achieve a complete congruence between life and art, for as he told *Time* magazine in May 1963: 'Paintings are too hard. The things I want to show are mechanical. Machines have less problems. I'd like to be a machine, wouldn't you?'

To achieve this machine-like end, after 1963 Warhol began to feign an almost robotic emotional and intellectual vacancy that was far removed from the sometimes overwrought and thinking persona that he revealed to his friends in private. It may be that coincidentally Warhol wanted to offset any public suspicions of his sexuality (for homosexuality was still widely unacceptable in America in the early 1960s, as both Jasper Johns and Robert Rauschenberg demonstrated by keeping their relationship extremely private) and such suspicions could easily have led to a refusal to take him seriously. But in any event his machine-like stance was certainly very effective in increasing media interest in him, for the more non-committal he appeared the more intriguing he became. As with the 'raggedy Andy' image he had cultivated during his early years in New York, Warhol was something of an actor as far as his behaviour was concerned, and always to very calculated effect. And the automatism also extended to his work-processes. Henry Geldzahler noted that in the early 1960s Warhol would paint 'with television sets going, and the contents of the pictures and the formal qualities – the black-and-white and the idea of repetition – came, I think, as much from watching television as anything else', while Ivan Karp recorded that when he first visited Warhol

there was a record playing . . . at an incredible volume . . . It was by Dickie Lee, called 'I Saw Linda

Yesterday'. And during the entire time I was there, [Warhol] did not take off the record and it played over and over again . . . I asked him why he did not change the record since there were other nice things to listen to, and I recommended other groups that might be interesting. He said that he really didn't understand these records until he heard them at least a hundred times.

But there was a serious purpose to this affectation of automatism, as Warhol himself made clear in his book *POPism: The Warhol '60s*:

> I still wasn't sure if you could completely remove all the hand gesture from art and become noncommittal, anonymous. I knew that I definitely wanted to take away the commentary of the gestures – that's why I had this routine of painting with rock and roll blasting the same song, a 45 rpm, over and over all day long – songs like the one that was playing the day Ivan came by for the first time, 'I Saw Linda Yesterday' by Dicky Lee. The music blasting cleared my head out and left me working on instinct alone. In fact, it wasn't only rock and roll that I used in that way – I'd also have the radio blasting opera and the TV picture on (but not the sound) – and if all that didn't clear enough out of my mind, I'd open a magazine, put it beside me, and half read an article while I painted. The works I was most satisfied with were the cold 'no comment' paintings.

Related to Warhol's affectation of a robotic stance in order to achieve and/or match the objectivity of his visual images was his affected avoidance of being taken seriously or even of taking himself seriously. His oft-quoted statement, first published in 1967, that 'If you want to know all about Andy Warhol, just look at the surface of

my paintings and films and me, and there I am. There's nothing behind it' is usually taken to signify that the artist did not intend any meanings whatsoever to reside in his works. But it is precisely in that very Nothingness that the artist's meanings reside, for it testifies to the meaning-lessness that Warhol saw in the world around him, a negation that gives his art its acute relevance to the spiritual emptiness in which Western man for the most part lives. Warhol was certainly a great dissembler when it came to verbal explanations of his works, for up until about 1963 many of his public statements were extremely specific about what he was attempting to communicate in his art (as we have already seen), whereas after that time he went out of his way to appear intellectually vacant, if not even simple-minded, about the meanings of his works, or even to deny that they bore any meanings at all, a denial that is contradicted by the power of his imagery and the ways that he employed it. Ultimately, Warhol's denial of meaning may be explained by his reluctance to limit the manifold implications of his works by verbal explanation, and by his suspiciousness of most critical dialogue, but that he remained unaware of what he was communicating seems unlikely. Indeed, all the available evidence points to his having been highly conscious of the nihilism he projected, not necessarily on his own behalf – for he definitely believed in God – but as a measure of what surrounded him.

Throughout the late spring and early summer of 1962 Warhol laboured on his canvases, making large pictures of individual soup-cans, teach-yourself-to-dance dia-grams and paint-by-numbers images. He also further extended his subject-matter by depicting serried ranks of Coca-Cola bottles, S & H Green Stamps, airmail stamps and stickers, and 'Glass – Handle with Care' labels. And simultaneously he moved in a different direction as well. On 4 June 1962 Warhol lunched at Serendipity with

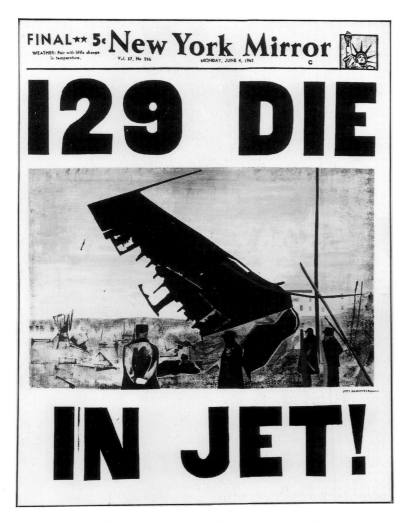

129 Die in Jet (Plane Crash), 1962, *Museum Ludwig, Cologne.*

reproduced on the left of the page. It was to be the first of many disaster pictures.

Yet in common with the other reproductions of newspaper front pages that Warhol made around this time, and many of the further works depicting objects in daily use that he was simultaneously producing, inevitably there is a sense of personal touch to the imagery which results from the fact that it is hand-painted and therefore not as mechanistic-looking as its prototypes. To counter this problem of unintended personality, and equally to help streamline the process of reproducing dollar bills, Coke bottles, Green Stamps, airmail stickers and the like *en masse*, several of these types of images were produced using handcut stencils or rubber stamps and wood blocks, all devices that Warhol had used in his former life as an illustrator. But his art took a huge technical step forward in July 1962 when Nathan Gluck suggested that if Warhol really wanted to cut out the laboriousness of producing repetitive images, he should use the photo-silkscreen printing technique instead.

With this method a photographic image is transferred to a screen of sensitized silk stretched on a frame, and the fine mesh of the silk permits ink or paint to pass through it onto a canvas or other support only where it is not protected by a membrane of resistant gum. The use of silkscreen printing meant that Warhol could now incorporate mechanical repetition directly into his work, rather than indirectly through painting each image slowly by hand, or by means of handcut stencils, stamps and blocks. It thus allowed him to address to the full the 'quantity and repetition' that he saw as being the essential content of his art, in addition to achieving that content through the 'assembly line effect' he wanted. Such a process also enjoyed the extra virtue of adding to the mechanical look of the image, although Warhol was careful to guard against that mechanization becoming too

Henry Geldzahler, who told him: 'That's enough affirmation of life . . . It's enough affirmation of soup and Coke bottles. Maybe everything isn't so fabulous in America. It's time for some death. This is what's really happening.' He then handed Warhol a copy of that morning's *Daily News* which carried the headline '129 DIE IN JET!' Once again Warhol immediately grasped the underlying cultural implications of such imagery and created the painting of the selfsame front page that is

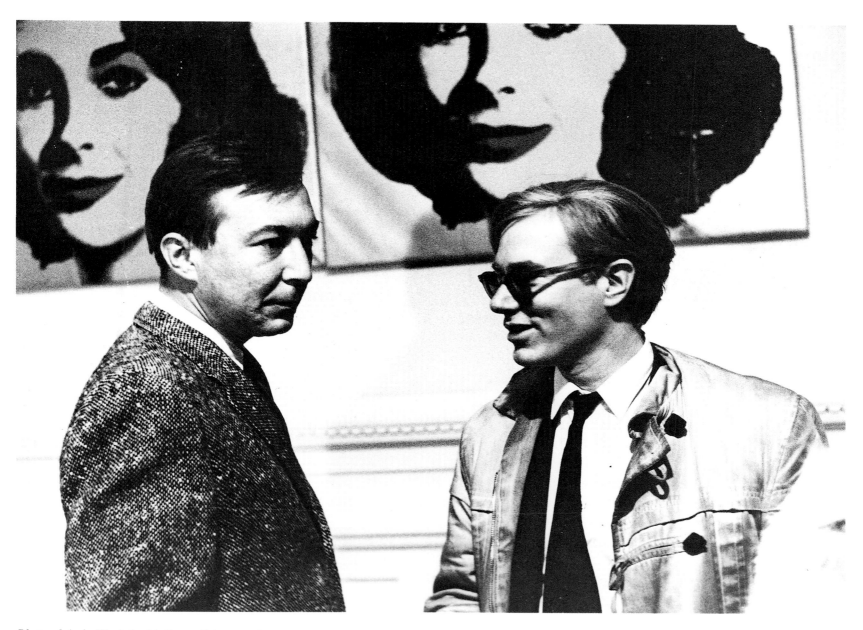

Photo of Andy Warhol with Jasper Johns, c.1964.

sterile by encouraging variations in inking. Moreover, this unevenness would introduce associations of the kind of unevenness that frequently occurs at the proofing stages of mechanical printing, evidence of which (in the form of colour proofs) Warhol had seen innumerable times during his commercial art career. Indeed, from the start (with the painting of *Baseball*, reproduced on page 55), Warhol employed the chance effects of silkscreen printing in order to bring directly into play a set of specific associations, for the overlaps and variations of tonal density exactly emulate the arbitrary overlaps and variations of tonal density of commercial printer's trial proof sheets. Clearly, Warhol apprehended such trial proofings as offering an alternative subject to the comic strips being dealt with contemporaneously through the emulation of dot techniques by Roy Lichtenstein. And equally, the overlaps and extreme tonal ranges of density in the inking add great visual variety, immediacy and suggested movement to the images. As a result of the use of photo-silkscreen, Warhol could now deal with a much vaster range of imagery, including the representation of people whose likenesses would have been much harder to arrive at accurately by hand, and the approximation of whose appearances would inevitably have introduced an unintended personality to the imagery through the necessary 'touch' of the artist when making the pictures. By using photo-silkscreen, Warhol the 'machine' came one step closer to achieving full realization, with the extra advantage that if necessary the artist could utilize the labour of others in order to help him create the images, as well as enable him to work easily on a comparatively vast scale.

For Warhol, July 1962 was also important for another reason: in that month he held his first one-man show as a fine artist. However, this debut was mounted not in New York but in Los Angeles, where the owner of the Ferus Gallery, Irving Blum, displayed the 32 Campbell's Soup paintings as an ensemble. The exhibition received only limited critical coverage, but it was moderately successful in terms of sales. Yet Blum soon repented of having sold any of the pictures, for belatedly he realized the artistic value of the ensemble and determined to keep it together; to that end he bought back the works he had parted with and purchased the entire set from Warhol for $1000, the money to be paid off at $100 per month.

Warhol did not travel to Los Angeles for the show, but the very day it ended (4 August 1962) Marilyn Monroe committed suicide, and so he immediately began a series of silkscreened pictures of her that were destined to become his most famous images. In the Marilyns series, Warhol heightened the garishness of the film actress's lipstick, eyeshadow and peroxide blonde hairdo, obviously to make points about the garishness of 'glamour' and stardom, while in many of the works repetitiveness played a crucial role, obviously to mirror the visual repetitiousness through which Marilyn Monroe had habitually been presented to the world. Once the Marilyns series was completed, Warhol used the silkscreen technique to create further sets of the soup-cans, Coke bottles, coffee-cans and dollar bills images that he had so laboriously painted earlier that year, as well as embarking upon new sets of images of movie and pop stars such as Elizabeth Taylor, Marlon Brando and Elvis Presley.

All this hard work soon paid off, for in the summer of 1962 Warhol was at last promised a show in New York, to be held at Elinor Ward's Stable Gallery on West 58th Street in November. A foretaste of what the public would see there came at the end of October when Warhol exhibited four of his works in a group Pop Art show, entitled 'The New Realists', at the Sidney Janis Gallery. Amidst works by Roy Lichtenstein, James Rosenquist, Claes Oldenburg and another great many other American and European artists, Warhol exhibited a big painting of a

Campbell's soup-can; a picture bringing 200 Campbell's soup-cans together in ten ranks of 20 cans; a *Do-it-yourself* painting; and one of the Dance Diagram pictures which was exhibited under glass on the floor, with a label attached inviting members of the public to remove their shoes and follow the dance steps on the painting itself (the joke was compounded by the fact that Sidney Janis was an enthusiastic dancer). This show created a sensation and it set the seal on the new direction that art was taking, although naturally the preceding generation of New York artists, for whom painting was a decidedly serious business, were profoundly shocked by it. And just a week later, on 6 November 1962, Warhol finally made his New York debut with his Stable Gallery show. On view were 18 pictures, including the *Gold Marilyn*, *129 Die in Jet*, another Dance Diagram painting that was again placed on the floor with an invitation to dance over it, the highly repetitive *Red Elvis* and several Coca-Cola bottles and soup-can pictures. The exhibition was an almost total sell-out, for it generated enthusiastic responses that were worthy of the artist's highest aspirations down the years. Never again during his lifetime would Warhol leave the public eye.

In February 1963 the Metropolitan Museum of Art in New York put Leonardo da Vinci's *Mona Lisa* on display for a month, and Warhol thereupon made some paintings incorporating the image, one of which is reproduced on page 85. These pictures not only debunk the cultural status of the Leonardo but equally stress the vast mass-media dissemination of the original image. In May 1963, when racial tension in the American South was at its height due to the struggle for black civil rights, Warhol developed a series of paintings of police dogs savaging blacks in Birmingham, Alabama; he went on throughout the rest of that year to explore the related implications of deaths and disasters in a long series of images of suicides,

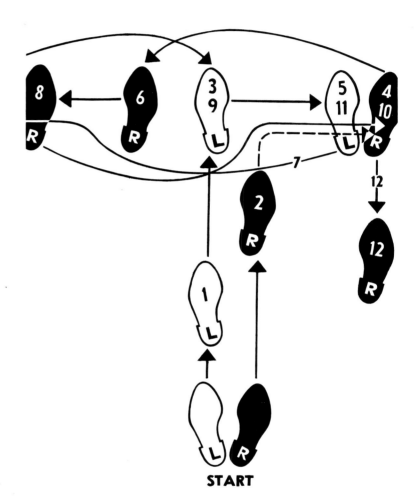

Dance Diagram – Tango, *1962, Museum of Modern Art, Frankfurt-am-Main, Germany.*

car crashes, gangster funerals, electric chairs, fatalities caused by food poisoning, atomic explosions and, from December 1963, Jackie Kennedy at the presidential funeral of her husband less than a month earlier. As the painter related to Gene Swenson soon after he had embarked upon this series of works:

I realized that everything I was doing must have been Death. It was Christmas or Labor Day – a holiday –

and every time you turned on the radio they said something like, '4 million are going to die.' That started it. But when you see a gruesome picture over and over again, it doesn't really have any effect. The death series I did was divided in two parts: the first on famous deaths and the second on people nobody ever heard of and I thought that people should think about some time: the girl who jumped off the Empire State Building or the ladies who ate the poisoned tuna-fish and people getting killed in car crashes. It's not that I feel sorry for them, it's just that people go by and it doesn't really matter to them that someone unknown was killed so I thought it would be nice for those unknown people to be remembered.

As well as addressing our indifference to the deaths of people unknown to us, in almost all of Warhol's Death and Disaster pictures the visual repetitiousness makes cultural points about the way we habitually encounter tragic or horrific imagery through the mass media, whilst the fact that most of us find such imagery intriguing throws back in our faces the morbidity, vicariousness or prurience of our interest in disaster. The use of colour also importantly contributes to the associations of such imagery, as does the fact that Warhol coupled many of the paintings with a complementary canvas painted blankly with the same background colour. Ostensibly he did so to give purchasers of the works twice as much painting for the same money, but behind this apparently cynical motive it is possible to detect another, more darkly thought-provoking and completely serious rationale: the blankness of each complementary image projects the cosmic meaninglessness of the accidental or man-made tragedies that are represented alongside.

By mid-1963 working conditions in the house in Lexington Avenue had become much too crowded, so in order to create yet more pictures, and on a bigger scale, in June of that year Warhol first rented additional studio space in an abandoned firehouse at East 87th Street and then, in the following November, he took over a vast loft at 231 East 47th Street which henceforth became known as 'The Factory' because it had previously been a hat factory. One of his helpers, Billy Name, painted the whole interior with silver paint or decorated it with silver foil, and Warhol liked the effect for the associations it held with space ships and the silver screens of old Hollywood movies. In order to speed up his work, that summer the painter took into his employ another studio assistant, Gerard Malanga, and because of such help he was soon able to free himself sufficiently to begin making movies.

The artist had not been overly impressed with the underground films that were then beginning to circulate in large numbers, so in July 1963 he bought a small Bolex cine camera for $1200 and soon afterwards he made the first of his many movies, *Sleep*. This lasted for six hours and it simply showed his current boyfriend, John Giorno, in a deep slumber. Initially Warhol ruined all the footage of *Sleep* through unloading the camera wrongly and thus he had to shoot the film all over again, but eventually he got the hang of things, and was excited by the potential of the medium. A typical film of the period is *Empire* which shows the outside of the Empire State Building over an eight-hour period from twilight to the early hours of the morning; the building is not apparent for the first two reels of the movie due to over-exposure of the film. In films like *Sleep* and *Empire*, as well as in his many other movies made in 1963–4 such as *Kiss*, *Haircut*, *Eat*, *Dracula*, *Couch*, *Drunk*, *Hand Job* and *Blow Job*, what Warhol sought to project was a mechanical, emotionally detached statement, with as little intervention of the creator as possible – indeed, for several of these films he

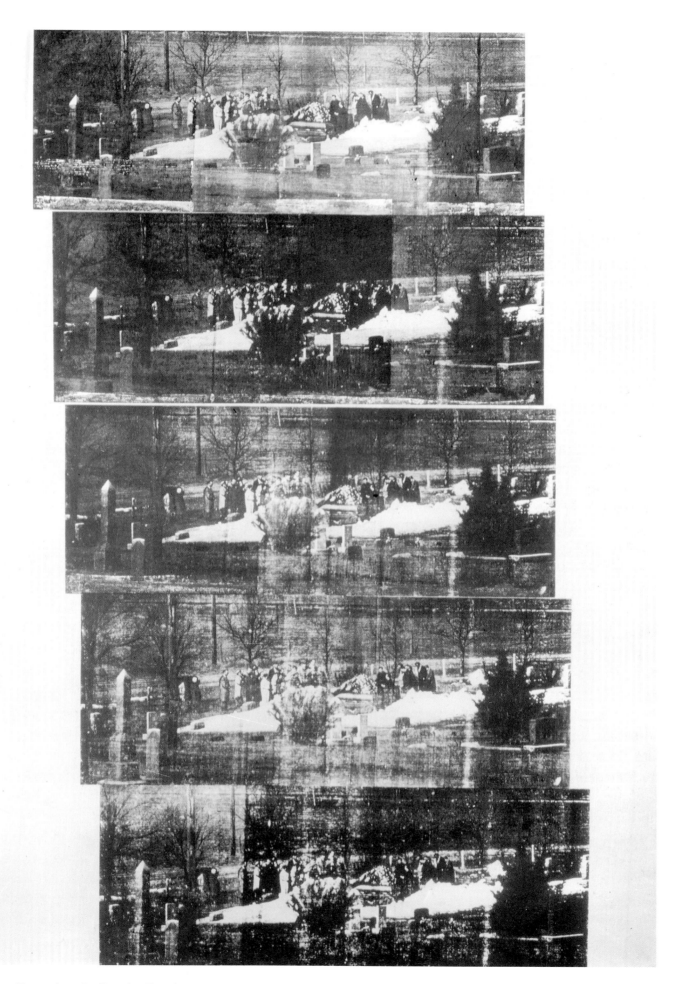

Gangster Funeral, *1963, Dia Art Foundation, New York.*

would set up the camera and then make telephone calls elsewhere whilst the filming was taking place. Such films do not necessarily enjoy a one-to-one temporal relationship with the real world, for Warhol slowed down their projection speeds so as to slow down their action in order to make it clear that 'When nothing happens, you have the chance to think about everything.' In this respect he was anticipating the minimalist absence of visual stimulus and action that would become so artistically widespread a decade or so later. His innovations were certainly hailed by some of his more experimentalist contemporaries, for they awarded him the annual prize of the New York underground movie magazine *Film Culture* at the end of 1964.

In September 1963 Warhol held a second exhibition at the Ferus Gallery in Los Angeles, this time showing a series of Elvis Presley paintings in one room of the gallery, and 12 pictures of Elizabeth Taylor in the other. Tempted by the promise of a Hollywood party to be held in his honour by the actor Dennis Hopper, by the fact that 'Vacant, vacuous Hollywood was everything I ever wanted to mould my life into. Plastic. White-on-white' and by other attractions such as the opening in the same week of nearby art exhibitions by Marcel Duchamp and Claes Oldenburg, Warhol persuaded three friends to drive him out to California for the opening. However, despite the popular subject-matter of his paintings and their comparatively low prices, the Ferus Gallery show was not a success, with bad reviews and no sales. And back in New York Warhol subsequently had trouble with Elinor Ward as well, for she hated the Disaster pictures and refused to exhibit them; as a result, the painter, who was at the height of his powers, had no showing at all of his works in New York in 1963. The Disasters, however, were soon acclaimed elsewhere, as happened in Paris in January 1964 when Warhol had his first European exposure at the

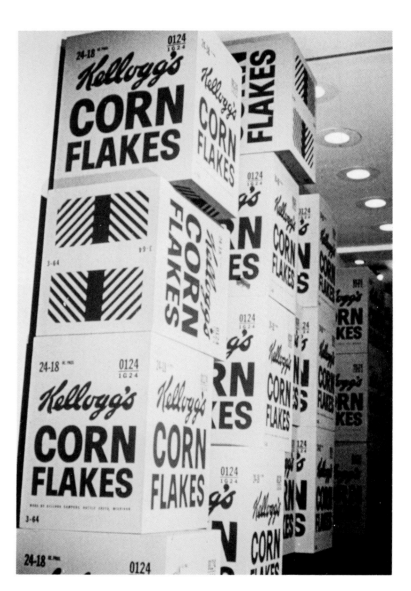

Photo of Boxes *at Stable Gallery, 1964.*

Ileana Sonnabend Gallery, where he displayed a group of them under the title of *Death in America*. But faced with the problems he was encountering with Elinor Ward in New York, Warhol upped his artistic ante by producing a set of objects that would not perhaps ostensibly look as shocking as the Disaster paintings, but which in cultural terms would make them appear tame by comparison.

These objects were six vast sets of reproduction outer packing cartons, of the type that serve to transport commodities from factories to supermarkets. When Warhol exhibited them in April 1964 at the Stable Gallery he filled the space virtually from floor to ceiling with over 400 of the works, thus making the gallery look exactly like a supermarket store-room. The packing-carton sculptures greatly furthered the statements that Warhol had already made in his paintings about mass culture and mass production, the imagery of packaging and the mechanization of imagery, as well as advancing the assaults on fine-art values those statements represented, and within the context of an art gallery equally they pointed up the very commercialization of art itself. Yet although the show received enormous critical coverage – for Warhol had yet again accurately predicted the shock value of what he was doing – and Robert Scull ordered some of the works (he later rescinded the order), sales were generally poor and the exhibition caused a final rupture between Ward and Warhol, who thought the dealer was insufficiently supportive. Thereafter the artist moved to the Leo Castelli Gallery.

Photo of Warhol's Flowers *exhibition at the Leo Castelli Gallery, New York, 1964.*

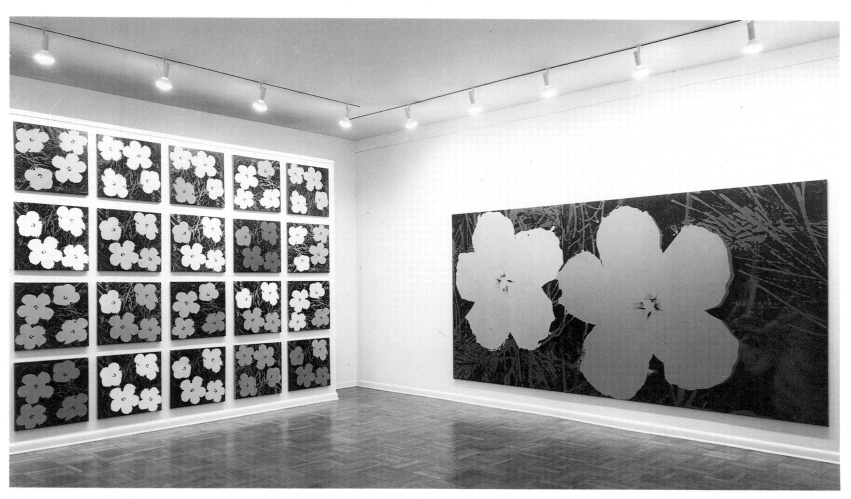

By the time the carton sculptures exhibition opened, to some controversy, Warhol had anyway stirred up controversy elsewhere in New York by creating a mural for the New York State Pavilion at the World's Fair in Flushing Meadow Park. This comprised a series of blown-up police mug-shots of criminals but the work was deemed to be libellous and Warhol was therefore asked to remove it, although rather than do so he simply had it painted over. Warhol's innate desire to confound expectations surfaced yet again in his next New York exhibition, held at the Leo Castelli Gallery in November 1964. Once more the painter had taken Henry Geldzahler's advice on subject-matter, for just as the art curator had motivated him into dealing with death and disaster in 1962, so now he felt that Warhol had painted enough gloom-laden pictures and should paint flowers instead. Naturally there was nothing offensive about such imagery, and it may be that Warhol responded with alacrity to Geldzahler's suggestion because the public might prove to be more financially receptive to pictures of flowers than they had been to reproductions of supermarket artefacts or images of death and disaster. In the event, the show was a complete sell-out, which Warhol must have doubly welcomed, for as a painter he had never yet matched his income as a commercial designer in the 1950s.

As 'Art' became an increasingly glamorous (and financially attractive) activity in New York during the 1960s, and as the word got about regarding Warhol's extreme amenability to employing virtually anyone in his films, so the number of helpers and hangers-on at the Factory greatly expanded. As Robert Hughes has succinctly defined them, 'They were all cultural space-debris, drifting fragments from a variety of sixties subcultures (transvestite, drug, S&M, rock, Poor Little Rich, criminal street, and all the permutations) orbiting in smeary ellipses around their unmoved mover.' Many of these people suffered drug-related emotional or mental problems, but Warhol welcomed such social misfits (at least until he was shot by one of them in 1968), obviously because they were extremely susceptible to manipulation by him as leader of the pack. Increasingly the artist derived a peculiar satisfaction from exercising sexual and/or psychological control over them and, as the underground movie actor Taylor Mead commented, 'The more destroyed you were, the more likely [Warhol] was to use you.' Just how cynical he could be in his dealings with his entourage is demonstrated by an incident that occurred in October 1964 when one of his hangers-on, Freddie Herko, committed suicide by jumping from a fifth-floor window in Greenwich Village whilst high on LSD: Warhol was heard to complain repeatedly that Herko should have forewarned him so that he could have filmed the death.

Coupled with Warhol's manipulativeness was his lifelong need for the psychological buttressing that can only be obtained through exaltation by others. Such a compulsion for fame certainly explains the painter's love of partying (or what he called his 'Social Disease'), for even in his early days in New York, Warhol was never happy unless he had a party to go to every night, and in time he would move this love onto a more structured plane via his magazine *Interview*, which gave him a means of social access to any party in the land, including presidential parties. Yet some of the worst artists in history have been moral purists, and some of the best have been complete social misfits, and much recent intellectual confusion and pompous moral outrage has been directed at Warhol's work because of his social behaviour. This is unfortunate, for as George Orwell once commented upon Salvador Dalí (who also created moral outrage in his heyday), it should be possible to hold in one's head simultaneously

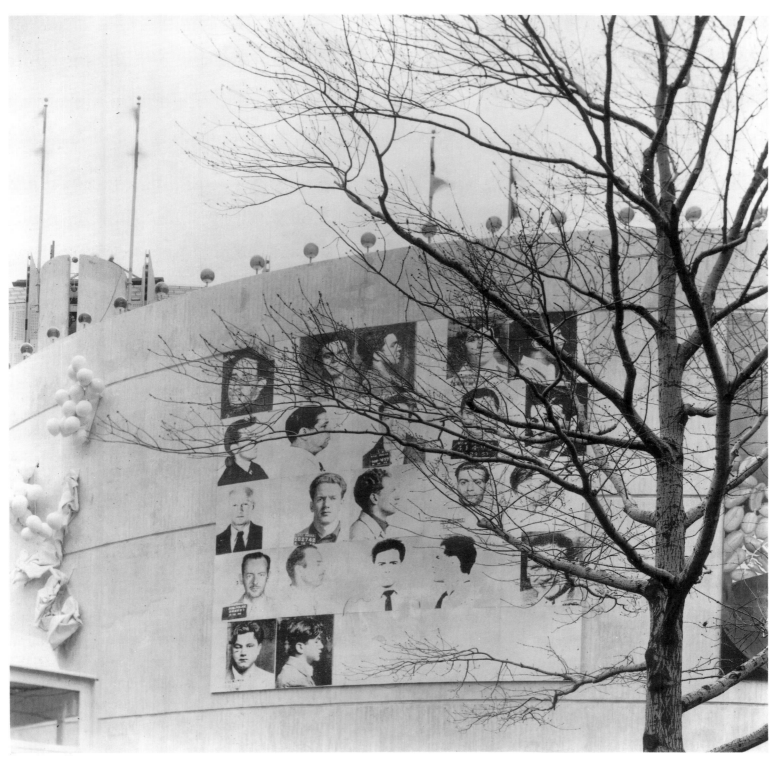

Photo of exterior of New York State pavilion at New York World's Fair,
1964, showing Warhol's Thirteen Most Wanted Men *in situ.*

the two facts that someone is a good artist and a disgusting human being; the one does not cancel out the other. Warhol was not very disgusting – at worst he was just a creep – but his art is something apart from that, or should be regarded as such. And whilst he undeniably created a great deal of art cynically in the 1970s and 1980s, some of the work made in those decades is not cynical at all and should not be condemned with the rest – it is always necessary to sort the artistic wheat from the chaff, as we shall attempt to do in these pages.

In January 1965 Warhol designed a *Time* Magazine cover using photo-booth pictures of assorted youths for a story on 'Today's Teenagers'; he had previously employed such photos in 1963 for his memorable portrait of Ethel Scull (reproduced on page 83), and again they introduced a note of downbeat immediacy to the proceedings. At the end of April 1965 Warhol flew to Europe for the first time. His initial stop was Paris for a display of the *Flowers* paintings at the Ileana Sonnabend Gallery, and thereafter he visited London and Madrid before going on with a small group of friends to that mecca of gays and soft-drug users, Tangiers. After his return to New York in June Warhol created further films, including *Screen Test #1*, *The Life of Juanita Castro*, *Horse*, *Vinyl*, *Kitchen*, *Beauty #2*, *My Hustler*, *Bitch* and *The Death of Lupe Velez*. From the making of *My Hustler* onwards the films began to look and sound more like professional movies, with the use of audible soundtracks and the rudiments of plotting and camerawork. This change was mainly due to the employment of Paul Morrissey, who would prove increasingly important to Warhol's filmic activities because of his understanding of the basics of cinematic technique. Due to Warhol's increased involvement in film-making in 1965, the artist did little painting that year, although he did produce a new set of Campbell's Soup-Can paintings in which he rang the colour

changes upon the normal appearance of those objects. That October he also enjoyed his first one-man museum retrospective exhibition at the Institute of Contemporary Art in Philadelphia, and the opening turned into a near-riot due to the vast numbers of people who turned up simply to catch a glimpse of Warhol himself – the artist as cultural superstar. Paradoxically, when and if those people did get into the museum there was little for them to see, as the curator had had most of the paintings removed lest they be damaged in the crush. Probably the bare walls seemed like one of Warhol's anti-artistic stratagems to most of those present.

By the end of 1965 Warhol was again beginning to run out of ideas. One day he got into conversation with Ivan Karp:

> Warhol said that he was using up images so fast that he was feeling exhausted of imagination . . . he said, 'I'm running out of *things* . . . Ivan, tell me what to paint!' And he would ask everybody that. He asked Henry [Geldzahler] that. He asked other people that he knew. He asked, 'What shall I paint? What's the subject?' I couldn't think of anything. I said, 'The only thing that no one deals with now these days is pastorals . . . My favourite subject is cows.' He said, 'Cows . . . Of course! Cows! New cows! Fresh cows!'

At the artist's behest, Gerard Malanga then found a suitable bovine image in an old agricultural magazine, and subsequently this was made up as wallpaper, which was used to cover the walls of one of the two rooms in Warhol's next exhibition held at the Leo Castelli Gallery in April 1966. With its particularly dumb look, the image brings to an absurd end the pastoral tradition in Western art, and it also fixes Warhol's negative view of picture-making by 1966, for by then the artist was disillusioned

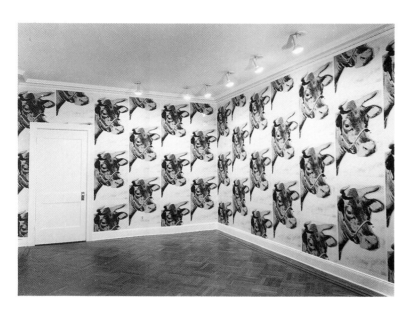

Photo of installation of Cow Wallpaper *at Leo Castelli Gallery, New York, 1966.*

with the creation of fixed images. The installation undoubtedly projected his view that the only remaining role for wall-hung works of art was as decorative wallpaper; as he stated, when asked whether homes or art galleries provided better settings for his pictures: 'It makes no difference – it's just decoration.' That view is understandable in the mass culture in which we live, for indubitably paintings and their reproductions are mostly used these days as just so much decorative wall-covering.

The other half of the 1966 Castelli Gallery show consisted of a roomful of silver, helium-filled balloons called *Silver Clouds* that floated around aimlessly. Initially Warhol had wanted these objects to be floating light-bulbs – he owned a drawing of a horizontally-reclining light-bulb by Jasper Johns – but this did not prove to be technically feasible and so he settled on the more easily realizable pillow-shaped forms instead. They were certainly at the aesthetic cutting edge of sculpture at the time, for they were linked to contemporary developments in kinetic sculpture and, by dint of the fact that spectators could touch them, in participatory sculpture as well (indeed, in 1968 Merce Cunningham would use the objects in his ballet *Rain Forest*). Warhol said of them:

I didn't want to paint any more so I thought that the way to finish off painting for me would be to have a painting that floats, so I invented the floating silver rectangles that you fill up with helium and let out of your windows.

Warhol also claimed that the *Silver Clouds* were intended for people with too many possessions, who only had to let the balloons float away and thereby have one less object to worry about. Naturally, both the Cow Wallpaper and the balloons (which periodically had to be refilled with helium) were hardly conducive to mass sales, and financially the show was not a great success. As a consequence, Warhol did not exhibit again at the Castelli Gallery for another eleven years.

The 1966 exhibition marked the end of Warhol's finest period as a visual artist, for between then and the early 1970s the focus of his creative interests moved elsewhere, as we shall see. But before we pursue the painter's subsequent development, it is worth briefly surveying the types of artistic statement he had made between 1961 and 1966.

With the exception of the packing carton and *Silver Clouds* sculptures, which obviously related to the anti-art gestures of earlier masters of Dadaism such as Marcel Duchamp, it is possible to divide the majority of works created between 1961 and 1966 into two clear categories. First there are the iconic images. These are the consumer-object works, such as the soup-can or Coke-bottle pictures and the paintings of movie stars or of 'most wanted men'. In such images Warhol was obviously inspired by the way that Jasper Johns had intensified the iconic qualities of the American flag by isolating it frontally and setting it amid a field of flat colour; Warhol similarly isolated and set his objects or people so as to project them as solitary or multiplicatory icons, albeit icons of American popular culture (into this category the electric chair pictures may also be fitted). Then there are the situation pictures, such as the paint-by-numbers and the Deaths and Disasters paintings. Here the original visual material on which the works were based was less well-disposed to such iconic projection simply because it is more visually asymmetric, and in any case the imagery itself projects dramatic situations, rather than static or passive ones. Of course, in both categories of works the repetition of the imagery carries cultural implications pertaining to mass communications, as does the mechanical appearance of things, as already discussed. And between 1961 and 1966 this imagery had touched upon a vast range of activity and experience: mass-production and commercialization; money-worship and media-worship; the superficialities of the mass-communication media; criminality, death and disaster (from domestic disasters to atomic annihilation); and the natural world, both as flora and fauna. Warhol's increasing disillusion with fixed images by 1966 was therefore probably inevitable, given that he had used up subject-matter 'so fast that he was feeling exhausted of imagination'. Where could he go next?

Faced with this exhaustion, Warhol turned to other forms of cultural expression. In December 1965 he took over the rock music band Velvet Underground, and in April 1966 he made this group, along with the singer Nico, the centrepiece of a multimedia music show entitled the Exploding Plastic Inevitable that he opened at the Polish Cultural Center (or 'Dom') on St Mark's Place in New York. The show was in the vanguard of mid-1960s psychedelic rock-music displays, with the band performing against a backdrop of Warhol films and with strobe lighting adding to the constant visual bombardment. In May 1965, Warhol travelled to the West Coast for a tour with the Exploding Plastic Inevitable, but the trip turned into a disaster due to trouble with the police, the unions and hostile fellow-musicians. Back in New York, Warhol embarked upon his first commercially successful film, *Chelsea Girls*, and here again he made evident his desire to open up new visual experiences, for several reels of the movie were designed to be projected side-by-side at the same time and each with a different soundtrack. This film was generally well received when it opened in New York in September 1966, and it took so much money over the next few years that Warhol was able to subsidize his subsequent film-making from it, rather than rely upon the sale of paintings for that purpose.

Much of Warhol's time during the next year or so was taken up with Velvet Underground and with his filmic activities. The painter designed the cover of the Velvet Underground album, with a banana-peel sticker pulling off to reveal a flesh-coloured banana beneath, and in May 1967 he visited Cannes for a planned film festival screening of *Chelsea Girls*, although the movie was not shown in competition. Warhol then visited Paris and London before returning to New York and embarking upon further films, including *I, a Man* (featuring Valerie Solanas, who would figure importantly in Warhol's life the following year) and *Bikeboy*. But as far as his fine-art activities were involved, by 1967 Warhol's career was further on the wane. Again he sought help from outside, for as Ivan Karp later recalled, Warhol complained:

'Ivan, there's nothing left for me.' He said, 'I'm a popular character . . . but I've got no images.' I said, 'What's left for you? Do yourself.'

The result was a group of self-portraits that, intentionally or not, make the point that Warhol had himself become a cultural icon by 1967. This was soon borne out by the fact that the works came to be amongst the painter's most widely publicized images after he displayed six of them in the American Pavilion at the Montreal Expo '67 World's Fair. For these portraits Warhol clearly chose a photo taken when he was much younger, and they each enjoy highly inventive colour permutations and varieties of paint applications.

In 1967, also, Warhol made a further set of Electric Chairs paintings. But perhaps his biggest step forward that year as a fine artist was through his discovery of the creative and commercial potential of issuing large-scale sets of prints. He had earlier made one-off prints, but now he created a set of ten silkscreen-on-paper portraits of Marilyn Monroe in an edition of 250 portfolios. These prints once again demonstrate Warhol's remarkable powers as a colourist. The sets soon sold out, prompting the artist to pursue the creation of many more such portfolios, such as the group of 11 prints entitled *Flash – November 22, 1963* of 1968 which shows images relating to the assassination of President Kennedy, and the two sets of ten prints of Campbell's soups dating from 1968 and 1969 respectively. Such prints henceforth assured Warhol a good income from his work. To that end, and in terms of his earning potential, the artist's career took a further step forward in the autumn of 1967 when he engaged a professional business manager, Fred Hughes, who thereafter put the financing of the Andy Warhol empire on a new footing.

By now exhibitions of Warhol's work had burgeoned, as the artist's paintings came to be perceived as being amongst the most essential images of their time. Increasingly the painter was invited to lecture at various American universities but he dealt with that pressure in a typically insouciant way by hiring one of his entourage, Allen Midgette, to impersonate him; when the deception was discovered, Warhol was forced to return the lecture fees. Much of January 1968 was taken up with the making in Arizona of the pornographic comedy movie, *Lonesome Cowboys*, the creation of which led to Warhol being put under surveillance by the FBI. Soon afterwards the painter travelled to Stockholm for a retrospective exhibition at the Moderna Museet, the entire outside of which was covered with Cow Wallpaper for the occasion; if previously Warhol had used wallpaper to make a cultural point about art in domestic and gallery interiors, how much more effective and witty was that point when the wallpaper covered an entire museum on the outside.

In May 1968 Warhol travelled with Paul Morrissey to California to speak at further colleges (his past transgressions as a lecturer having been forgiven), and whilst in La Jolla they started yet another film, *Surfing Movie*, although police harassment and conflicts on the set prevented its completion. Back in New York, life at the Factory continued as hectically as ever, although by now Warhol had been forced to move his working premises to a new location at 33 Union Square West, as the old factory site was scheduled for demolition. But the change of workplace did little to alter the atmosphere of Warhol's creative surroundings, and certainly the move did nothing to diminish the inherent dangerousness of the painter's environment, stemming from its accessibility to people unbalanced by drugs or psychological problems. That incipient danger had certainly been brought home to Warhol on more than one occasion, as in 1964 when a hanger-on, Dorothy Podber, fired a gun through four stacked Marilyn canvases (works that were thereafter entitled the 'Shot Marilyn' pictures). Even more unnerving was an incident that occurred in November 1967, when a friend of one of Warhol's movie stars entered the studio with a gun: after playing Russian roulette with Paul Morrissey – fortunately the gun failed to go off, although it was fired into the ceiling immediately afterwards – he then forced Warhol to kneel at his feet before being prevailed upon to go away. But worse was to come less than a year later.

Late in the afternoon of 3 June 1968, Valerie Solanas, a mentally-ill actress, feminist and founder of a one-woman Society for Cutting Up Men (SCUM), walked into Warhol's studio and shot at the painter three times with a handgun. The third bullet passed right through him, badly injuring his gall-bladder, liver, spleen, and other vital organs *en route*. Solanas then shot the visiting art critic Mario Amaya, and threatened Fred Hughes, before being persuaded to leave; she gave herself up to a traffic cop later that day. (Subsequently she received a three-year prison sentence for the shooting.) Warhol was rushed to hospital where he was immediately operated on; fortunately the operation was successful, although the painter had to undergo further surgery the following year. He remained in hospital until 28 July and spent the rest of the year recuperating. Painting was one of his convalescent activities, and during the month after his discharge he worked on a multiple portrait of Happy Rockefeller. But unsurprisingly the failed murder attempt was to take its eventual psychological toll on Warhol by greatly heightening his feeling that both life and art are senseless.

That autumn the artist oversaw the production of his next movie, *Flesh*. This was directed by Paul Morrissey and was intended to be a more sexually explicit version of the John Schlesinger film *Midnight Cowboy* that was then being made in New York. Later that year Warhol also produced *Blue Movie*, which was openly semi-pornographic and exploitative, being a means of generating cash quickly, for the medical care stemming from the painter's shooting had cost a fortune and he was low on funds. And in order to make even more and quicker money, in the summer of 1969 Warhol moved yet further into the pornographic film business by mounting a season of hardcore gay porno movies at a Manhattan cinema he rented for the purpose. Perhaps it was activities like these that led to the artist's failure to be taken seriously in Hollywood, which he visited twice in 1969, unsuccessfully, in search of funding for movies.

Warhol virtually gave up painting between 1969 and 1971, telling Emile de Antonio that 'The critics are the real artists, the dealers are the real artists too. I don't paint any more. Painting is dead.' Instead he increased his other activities, in the autumn of 1969 founding an underground movie magazine, *Andy Warhol's Interview*, and also producing his most commercially successful film, *Trash*. May 1970 saw the opening in Pasadena, California, of a large retrospective exhibition of his paintings that later travelled to Chicago, Eindhoven (Holland), Paris, London and New York, and for some of these shows Warhol used Cow Wallpaper as the backdrop to the hanging of the paintings. Such a background added greatly to the visual density of the exhibit and again made a witty point about museums as spaces that habitually hang cultural wallpaper. On 13 May 1970 Warhol had the pleasure of seeing one of his Soup-Can paintings fetch the highest price ever yet reached at auction for a work by a living American artist.

In the autumn of 1970 an increasingly frail Julia Warhola moved back to Pittsburgh, where she suffered a stroke the following February and died a year and nine months later, aged 80; Warhol did not attend her funeral, possibly out of indifference, for in her last years he had probably come to find her a burden. Her return to Pittsburgh in 1970 certainly freed him to travel more, and consequently in September 1970 he flew to Paris to make a movie, *L'Amour*. He also visited London for his exhibi-

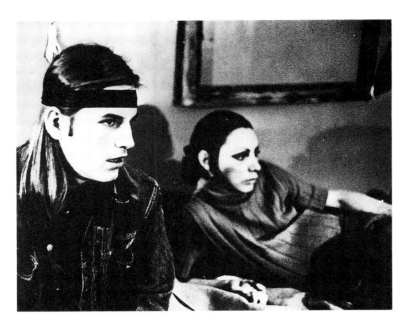

Still from the film Trash, *1970, showing Joe Dallesandro and Holly Woodlawn.*

tion at the Tate Gallery (which ran concurrently with three other Warhol shows in the city), as well as Cologne and Munich where he received the type of welcome usually reserved for pop musicians. That year Warhol made two movies, the first of which, *Women in Revolt*, was aimed at Valerie Solanas's feminism and women's liberation in general, whilst the second, *Heat*, was a send-up of Hollywood that was aptly made in Los Angeles itself, with Paul Morrissey directing and Sylvia Miles as the leading lady. In the autumn of 1970, *Pork*, a play that was based upon hours of taped conversations between Warhol and his studio entourage, was produced in New York and London.

Warhol made a welcome return to the visual arts in the winter of 1971–2 by creating over 2,000 paintings of the Chinese communist leader Chairman Mao. It was a masterstroke of irony on his part, for the politician represented everything that is antithetical to the American political, financial and cultural systems, whilst the

vast proliferation of such images (which were greatly increased in numbers by a Mao wallpaper that Warhol produced to hang as a backdrop for the exhibition) made highly relevant points about the worship of politicians and the proliferation of idolizing images of them. The Chairman Mao series was not Warhol's only political statement in the early 1970s; in 1972 the artist also created a painting and print series of lurid images of Richard Nixon, as a way of trying to frighten people into supporting the presidential campaign of Nixon's opponent, George McGovern. Here Warhol was following the example of Ben Shahn, who in 1964 had appealed for votes for Lyndon B. Johnson similarly by portraying Johnson's political opponent rather hideously. (To the end of his days Warhol was convinced that Nixon exacted a subtle revenge on him by getting the Internal Revenue Service constantly to audit his financial affairs thereafter.)

Yet Warhol's true sympathies did not lie in the political arena; instead, he was much more alert to the glamour of politics, as well as the politics of glamour. By the mid-1970s *Interview* magazine was becoming highly successful as it sloughed off its old identity as a movie magazine and instead covered the unfolding Manhattan social scene. At the time, increasing affluence was taking the social narcissism and moral turpitude of wealthy New Yorkers to new lows, and Warhol was in the vanguard of that hedonistic, mindless sensibility. The artist frequented the 'in-crowd' discotheque, Studio 54; he cultivated contacts in the pop music world such as Bob Dylan, Mick Jagger and John Lennon; he hung around the White House and hobnobbed with doomed kings and dictators, such as the Shah of Iran and President Marcos of the Philippines; and money became more and more of a creative incentive to him as his lavish international lifestyle demanded constant refuelling. In his book *The Philosophy of Andy Warhol*, published in 1975, he stated:

Business art is the step that comes after Art. I started as a commercial artist, and I want to finish as a business artist. After I did the thing called 'art' or whatever it's called, I went into business art. I wanted to be an Art Businessman or a Business Artist. Being good in business is the most fascinating kind of art.

To that end Warhol now began making huge numbers of commissioned portraits of the wealthy and famous – all that was required was the $25,000 cover price (and further copies came cheaper, so why not buy a set?) – and by the mid-1970s such portraits were earning the painter well over a million dollars a year. Henceforth two main tracks would run parallel in Warhol's visual output: his society portraits, which are usually as vapid as his writings on social matters (his *Diary* must rank as one of the 50 most ineffably boring books ever published); and those sadly fewer but by no means negligible numbers of paintings and prints in which Warhol the master explorer of the artistic and social implications of mass culture still shone forth.

There is little point in chronicling Warhol's travels once he moved into the international jet-set in the early 1970s, for after that time his journeys became too numerous to be interesting except to those intrigued by details of international flight schedules (and in any case some of those movements are listed in the Chronology). More important biographical developments during these years were the further change of studio that took place in August 1974, as well as the transfer of Warhol's own living-quarters in late 1975. The studio move was to the third floor of an office building located at 860 Broadway, where a much more visually bland and security-conscious environment was created, whilst the residential change was to a six-storey, neo-Georgian house situated at 57 East 66th Street that dated from 1911, for which the

painter paid $310,000. In 1975 Warhol made portfolios of Mick Jagger portrait prints and the *Ladies and Gentlemen* series of prints of drag queens, neither of which are of much artistic interest. And in the spring of 1976 he produced a final movie, *Bad*. It was the most expensive of all his cinematic efforts but it did very poorly at the box office, and that failure put an end to Warhol's cinematic career. One might bemoan the fact that film-making had kept the artist from his canvases for so many years, but given the absence of fresh painterly ideas it is clear that it was a necessary activity for him, and in any case his visual creativity was undoubtedly stimulated by it.

Warhol's major artistic efforts in 1976 were his Hammer and Sickle, and Skulls series of paintings and prints. The Hammer and Sickle images add little if anything to the political and cultural ironies of the Chairman Mao series, although they are fairly inventive visually, given the characteristic shapes of the objects they represent. However, the Skulls did mark a notable addition to Warhol's subject-matter, for they not only introduce associations that Warhol found especially pertinent after his shooting in 1968 (although he had dealt with those implications earlier) but also they relate to a long tradition of *memento mori* images in Western art.

In 1977 Warhol made the Athletes, Torsos and American Indian pictures, as well as his Oxidation series of paintings. The Athletes were an unashamed attempt to make some quick money with which to recoup the losses on the film *Bad*, and comprised portraits of a number of leading sporting figures such as Muhammad Ali, Pele, Jack Nicklaus and Chris Evert; none of the images is particularly interesting. Nor are the Torsos, a group of studies of both male and female nudes that work at the interface of representation and abstraction but which are not especially stimulating in either mode. The *American Indian* is simply a portrait of Russell Means who fought

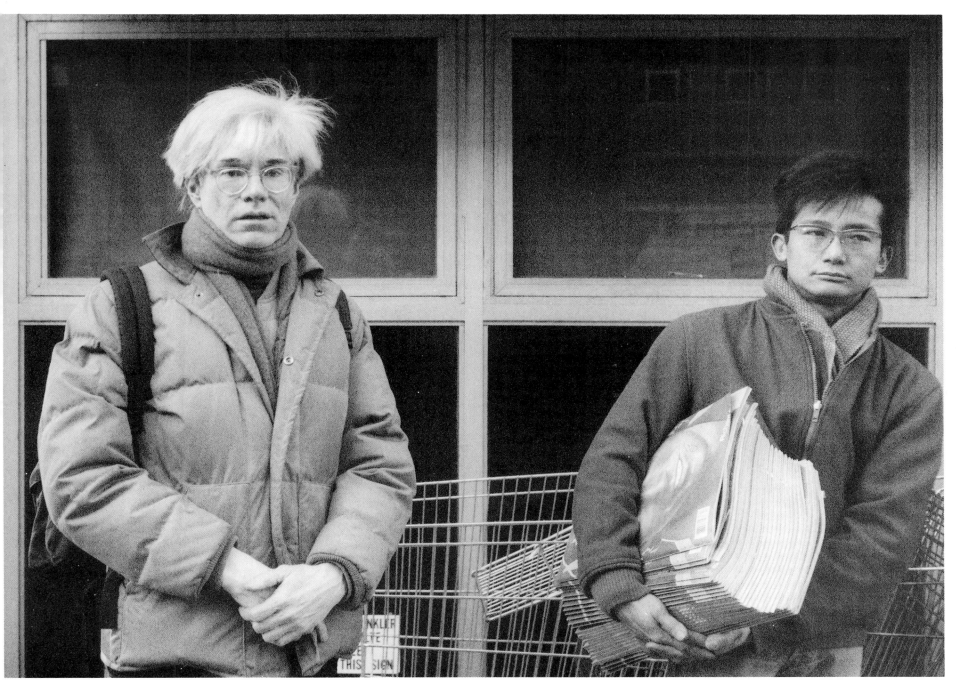

Andy Warhol distributing Interview *magazine on Madison Avenue, New York, 1983.*

for American Indian rights in the 1970s. And the Oxidation paintings perhaps represent the lowest conceptual and visual point that Warhol ever reached in his career, being a rather infantile anti-art gesture, of the type he had already made surreptitiously nearly 20 years earlier. The new pictures were made by coating canvases with copper paint onto which Warhol and his friends then urinated whilst the paint was still wet, so that the chemical interaction of the urine and paint caused the latter to oxidize (naturally, the paintings were not particularly nice to smell either). Such a process perhaps carries to a logical conclusion the implications of other urinary works of art in recent American art history, such as Marcel Duchamp's pissoir *Fountain* of 1917, or Claes Oldenburg's soft toilet, but Warhol's pictures do not enjoy anything of the wit of the two earlier works.

Warhol turned to male pornography in 1978 for the subject of his next group of images, the Sex Parts paintings and prints. Aesthetically and visually these works differ little from their original source material, the artist's intervention being just a few rather meaningless outlines superimposed over pornographic photo images. Far more challenging was his series of Shadows paintings. With the Oxidations and the Rorschach Test paintings of 1984, as well as a little-known series of explorations of the abstract potentialities of camouflage patterning made in the mid-1980s, these are Warhol's only abstract pictures, and although they are not particularly interesting individually, being in form superficially reminiscent of works by Franz Kline, they certainly make an effective point about the cultural proliferation of abstract art when they are exhibited *en masse*, as they were at the Heiner Friedrich Gallery in New York in 1979. And there is also a further level to these works which emerges when we consider them in the light of Warhol's next two series of pictures, the Reversals and the Retrospectives, both begun in 1978.

In both of these series Warhol recycled familiar images, perhaps, in the case of the Retrospectives, under the influence of Marcel Duchamp who had similarly surveyed his own earlier works in his *La Boîte en Valise*, two copies of which Warhol owned. The Reversals simply repeat the images used years before in works such as the Marilyns or the Mona Lisa paintings, except that they are now tonally reversed and look like photographic negatives. The Retrospectives comprise agglomerations of old Warhol images, sometimes in random arrangements or else in vertically-orientated series of visual strips identical to photo-booth vertical photographic strips, or which perhaps suggest strips of movie celluloid laid side-by-side. In all of these works Warhol characteristically explored new colour and tonal potentialities, but equally he offered a comment on himself that ties in more generally with his largely nihilistic outlook: the Reversals literally project a negative view of the painter's own artistic achievements, while the Retrospectives either offer a jumbled view of Warhol's achievements or else create associations of memory and processing, as though the art was simply something that had been processed *en masse*, which undoubtedly it had by 1979. And together these two series afford an additional insight into what Warhol may have been saying indirectly in the Shadows, for shadows are one of the oldest metaphors in existence for the negative and fleeting nature of things, that negativity and evanescence that lie behind the Reversals and Retrospectives series.

Andy Warhol continued to live in the fast lane during the late 1970s and 1980s. In 1979 he produced his own cable television programme, *Andy Warhol's TV*, and although this was broadcast weekly for about two years (and came back again later) it was commercially unsuccessful, for few people ever showed much interest in the artist's self-indulgent and narcissistic televisual approach to the world. Warhol travelled a great deal, and even made a trip to Iran in 1976; he published a book of vapid photographs of the international jet-set crowd, *Exposures*, for which he undertook a US and European promotional tour; he held a *Portraits of the Seventies* exhibition of depictions of his jet-set friends and clients at the Whitney Museum in New York at the end of 1979; and he launched into the 1980s by making a series of pictures entitled *Ten Portraits of Jews of the Twentieth Century*, images that include portrayals of Freud, Einstein, Gershwin, Martin Buber and the Marx Brothers but which unfortunately look like record album covers. Warhol hit another artistic low in November 1981 when he exhibited at the Los Angeles Institute of Contemporary Art alongside LeRoy Neiman, a kitsch, illustrative painter mostly employed by *Playboy* magazine (which underwrote the show). Yet at the same time Warhol painted a series of portraits of the German artist Joseph Beuys which make a very strong and witty cultural comment upon Beuys's status by covering his tonally reversed image with glittering artificial diamond dust, as though to play up the associations of showbiz glitter that Beuys enjoyed in the art world.

Warhol's next significant group of works dated from 1981, when he made the Dollar Signs, Knives, Guns and Myths series of paintings and prints. The first set returned to Warhol's favourite theme without adding much conceptually, although the array of $-signs does enjoy a certain visual wit. The Knives and Guns act as passive reminders of the American glamorization of violence, while the Myths series simply points up, yet again, the essential mythicality and cultural centrality of figures such as Mickey Mouse, Superman, Uncle Sam and even Warhol himself, who doubles in the pictures as a radio star, 'The Shadow', that he remembered from the 1930s.

In 1982 Warhol moved studios yet again, spending five million dollars on purchasing and renovating a redundant Consolidated Edison power plant situated at 32nd–33rd Streets between Madison and Fifth Avenues. In order to make that kind of money, the portraits industry rolled on in its fairly meaningless way, generating huge profits but rather worthless, if attractive images. But new additions to the oeuvre outside such easy works were the German Monuments series, showing a range of buildings, including ones erected by the Nazis; the straightforward Goethe pictures which simply recycle Wilhelm Tischbein's famous portrait of the great poet; and the De Chirico Replicas which repetitively point up the Italian painter's own visual repetitiousness. Further art-historical recycling took place in 1984, when Warhol reworked images by Edvard Munch (which led to his being sued for breach of copyright by the city of Oslo in Norway, the owner of the originals), and he also made pictures that feature details of Italian Old Master paintings; neither series do anything to improve upon their sources. Nor do the Rorschach Test series of paintings, for Warhol invented his own abstract patterns, unaware that Hermann Rorschach, the Swiss psychiatrist, had made uniform sets of such psychological testing patterns so as to be able to create uniform tests of responses. The images relate to recent developments in American abstract art but they achieve little else. And a further sign of Warhol's loss of daring and imagination by 1984 came in his short-lived artistic collaboration with two much younger but up-and-coming stars of the New York art scene, Francesco Clemente and Jean-Michel Basquiat. Both these artists rose to fame as a result of the 'post-modernist' exploration of graffiti and infantile imagery, and the works that Warhol made in collaboration with them seem a sloppy mishmash of styles, without any visual point or conviction. Life imitated art in its disconnection here, for by the time Warhol and Basquiat exhibited the fruits of their collaboration at the Tony Shafrazi Gallery in New York in September 1985, neither artist was on speaking terms with the other.

The quality of Warhol's art had become even worse by then, as he turned out an Advertisements series of paintings and prints in which he simply recycled ads for diverse products such as Chanel No.5 perfume and the Volkswagen Beetle. Attempts to add a little wit to the series by reproducing a Chinese design featuring James Dean or one of Ronald Reagan's old shirt adverts fell rather flat in the face of the evident prostitution of Warhol's talent: 'Business Art' it may have been, but it is a bad businessman who brazenly adulterates the quality of his own products. A series of Queens, this time not gay queens but female monarchs of England, Denmark, Holland and Swaziland, was made entirely by studio assistants following Warhol's instructions, although ultimately the artist himself must bear the responsibility for creating such dull images.

In 1986 Warhol made new but tired images of Lenin and of Frederick the Great; the former series covered exactly the same ironic ground as the Chairman Mao pictures, while the portrayals of Frederick the Great were commercially aimed at the highly lucrative German market, and say nothing about the great Prussian, either ironically or otherwise. Yet in 1986 there was also a return to form, for in his subsequent *Last Supper* paintings Warhol did have something to say about the way that great religious art can become cultural kitsch, whilst through using army camouflage patternings in several last self-portraits and other works (including a number of the *Last Supper* paintings), he found a way of creating interesting visual maskings that again project negation. In a final series of images, the sewn photographs of 1986–7, Warhol once more employed repetition and tonality, both to make familiar points about cultural repetition but equally to move recognizable imagery closer to abstraction. This had always been a positive quality of his art, ever since he had first become aware that repetition brings out the inherent abstraction of things.

By the end of 1986 Warhol's gallstones were increasingly causing him pain, although he refrained from doing anything about them because of his lifelong fear of doctors, hospitals and death. Early in January 1987 an exhibition of his stitched and sewn photographs opened to excellent reviews in New York, and soon afterwards he flew to Milan for an exhibition of his *Last Supper* paintings; as usual he was mobbed. Back in New York he created images of Rado Watches and of Ludwig van Beethoven, whilst planning the creation of yet another grandiose series of pictures, this time relating to the history of American television. But it was not to be. On 20 February Warhol checked into New York Hospital for a routine gall-bladder operation the following day. Although the operation itself was successful, the post-operative care was very lax and early on Sunday 22 February 1987 the painter died. He was just 59 years old.

His body was taken back to Pittsburgh where he was buried on 26 February; his tombstone was marked simply with his name and dates, even though he had once requested that it should be left blank or just bear the word 'figment'. In his will Warhol named Fred Hughes his executor and bequeathed him a quarter of a million dollars, the same sum that he left to each of his two brothers. The rest of his estate, valued at between $75 million and $100 million, went to create an arts charity, the Andy Warhol Foundation for the Visual Arts, which promises to be the richest such organization ever established in the United States.

By the end of his life Andy Warhol had become one of the leading mass-media personalities of his day and a touchstone of superficial contemporary social mores. But this should not blind us to his earlier seriousness and creative achievements. Certainly his career as a fine artist after the mid-1960s was uneven, but that seems inevitable, for between 1961 and 1966 the painter had explored most major aspects of modern experience and consequently had not left himself very much else to add. After that time he painted on more uncertain terms and with more uneven results, although occasionally he articulated something of importance, as with the Chairman Mao images of 1972 or the Reversals pictures of around 1980. And after 1968 Warhol seems understandably to have felt that he was living on borrowed time, so the nihilism and resulting shallowness of his latter days are surely explained by that realization. Yet despite all his apparent cynicism and his outward refusals to seem serious, Andy Warhol was far more than just a superficial Pop artist, for unlike many of his creative contemporaries his finest work is not simply about having fun in a mass culture: it confronts us with some of the underlying and most uncomfortable truths of our age, such as the inhumanity, exploitativeness, banality, trivialization and destructive-

ness of modern culture, as well as our loss of faith in God, art and life itself. Warhol may have wanted to appear to be a machine but under his apparent and assumed *sang-froid*, pretended intellectual vacancy and desire for fame there was an artist who did experience the pain of things considerably and expressed it subtly and cleverly in much of his work. (Indeed, the false imperturbability and mindlessness, and the pursuit of fame, were all evidently ways of staving off that pain.) Pain is expressible not only in tortured mouthings; it can be articulated by a detached voice, or even a hollow one. In Warhol's pictures of the material objects and other false idols that most of us worship, the pain lies just below the bright surfaces of the images and waits passively to engage us. If and when we take it seriously, the art of Andy Warhol has much to say about the perils that still confront us as we move into the next, even more highly manipulative and teeming millennium.

ERIC SHANES
LONDON, AUGUST 1990

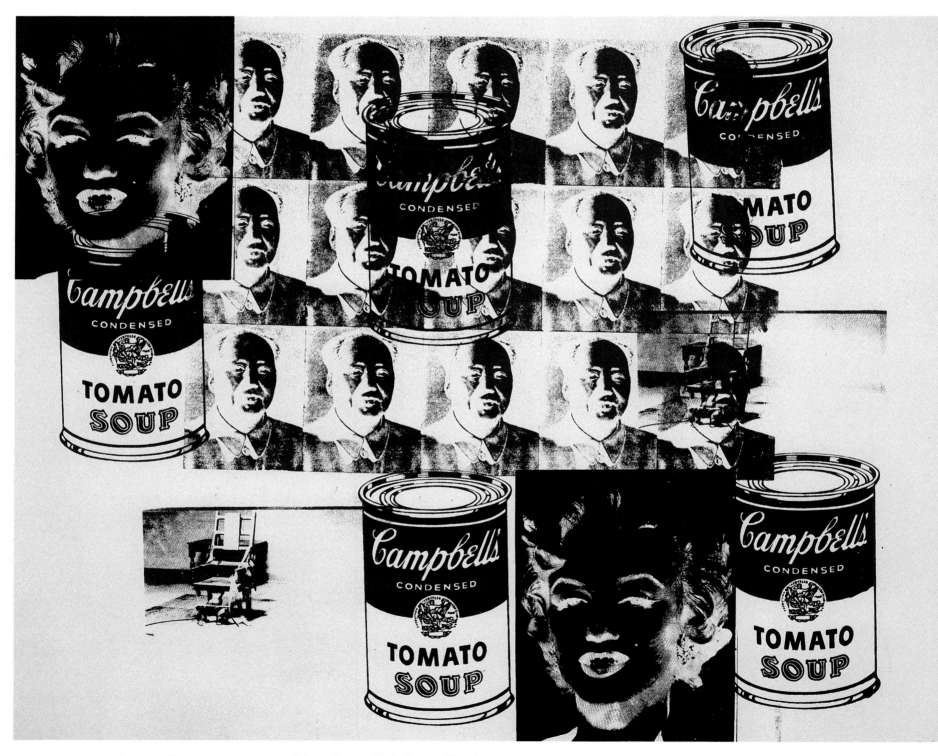

Black and White Retrospective, *1979, Galerie Bruno Bischofberger, Zurich.*

THE PLATES

Peach Halves, 1960

Synthetic polymer paint on canvas, 177.5 × 137.5 cm. Staatsgalerie, Stuttgart, Germany

Throughout 1960 and the following year Warhol became increasingly anxious to find the essential content of his art, without being able to do so, as the present work attests.

Here the painter was working at the interface between cultural and artistic statement by combining a subject-matter taken from popular culture with an abstract expressionist looseness of paint handling, very much in the conceptual wake of Jasper Johns and Robert Rauschenberg, if not necessarily in their manner. The result is neither fish nor fowl, offering only a limited statement about the cultural implications of a can of fruit, along with a rather flabby pictorial structure that does not enjoy to the full the courage of its visual convictions.

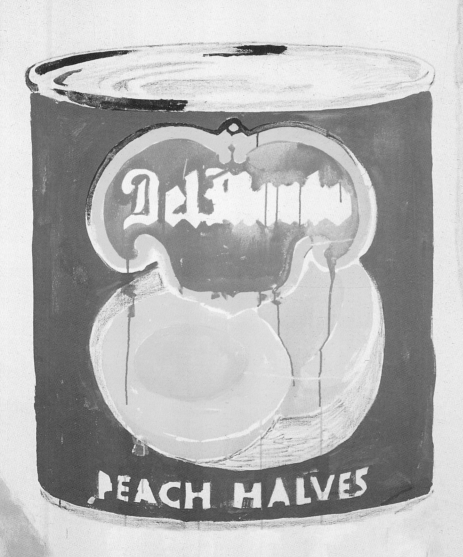

Saturday's Popeye, 1960

Synthetic polymer paint on canvas, 108.5 × 98.7 cm. Neue Galerie, Sammlung Ludwig, Aachen

This is one of the works that Warhol displayed in April 1961 in a 57th Street window of the Bonwit Teller department store in New York, where it received little if any attention.

Along with the crudely drawn representationalism that Warhol appropriated from cheap advertisements in works like *Peach Halves*, comic-strip imagery was another obvious visual source with which he tried to find some new way forward for his art in 1960. In this picture the artist again combined popular imagery with a quasi-expressionist paint handling that lacks conviction: the drips look rather too artificial to be witty, and they certainly do not signify painterly commitment, as they might have done in works by the more serious abstract painters of the New York school of the preceding generation. Here Warhol greatly simplified his source material so as to bring it nearer to abstraction, and indeed, it was his responsiveness to the inherent abstract qualities of form that would greatly strengthen his mature pictures as well. But although this work enjoys some formal impact, it offers little cultural comment, and certainly it says nothing about the production values of mass-communications media imagery that, unbeknown to Warhol when he made the work, his contemporary Roy Lichtenstein was beginning to explore more forcibly at the time through his adoption of Ben Day dot stencils, in order to emulate the dot patternings of mechanically printed newspaper reproductions. Only when Warhol learned of Lichtenstein's exploration of comic strips did he abandon such subject-matter, and as he wrote later in his book *POPism: The Warhol '60s*:

> Ivan [Karp showed] me Lichtenstein's Ben Day dots and I thought, 'Oh, why couldn't *I* have thought of that?' Right then I decided that since Roy was doing comics so well, that I would just stop comics altogether and go in other directions where I could come out first – like quantity and repetition.

The final part of this statement is highly revealing, both of Warhol's desire to proclaim his own personality independently of Lichtenstein, and of what he saw as his essential subject-matter. However, as we have noted in the Introduction (p. 16), it would not be until the end of 1961, and then as the result of a chance conversation, that the painter would eventually discover the imagery and cultural comment that would take him forward as an artist.

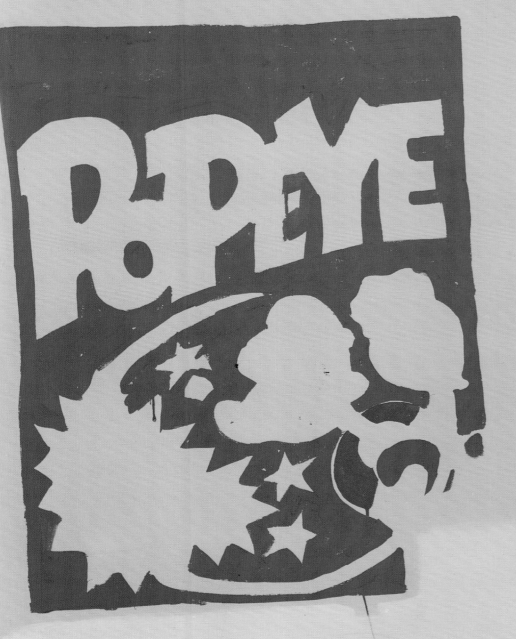

Before and After 3, 1962

Synthetic polymer paint on canvas, 182.9 × 255.9 cm. Whitney Museum of American Art, New York

This is a more refined version of an earlier and somewhat more expressionistically painted picture that Warhol exhibited in the Bonwit Teller department store window in 1961. That work includes arbitrarily cut-off words and long paint-drips running messily down the canvas, features that rather ruin its visual impact, for as Warhol subsequently realized, the image has no need of words, and its humorousness is surely increased by being presented in a totally deadpan way.

Cultural banality is the underlying theme here, as a crude juxtaposition derived from a magazine small-ads section underlines the pettiness of human vanity by reminding us that a straight or concave (i.e. inwardly curving) nasal profile is generally considered to be more appealing than a convex one. (Moreover, the joke is a double one, for of course in 1956 Warhol himself had had an operation on his rather bulbous nose to make it less ugly, an adjustment that was unsuccessful.) And ultimately the work deals with the concept of physical attractiveness, and how it may be artificially created, concerns that stand at the very heart of both mass culture and art itself.

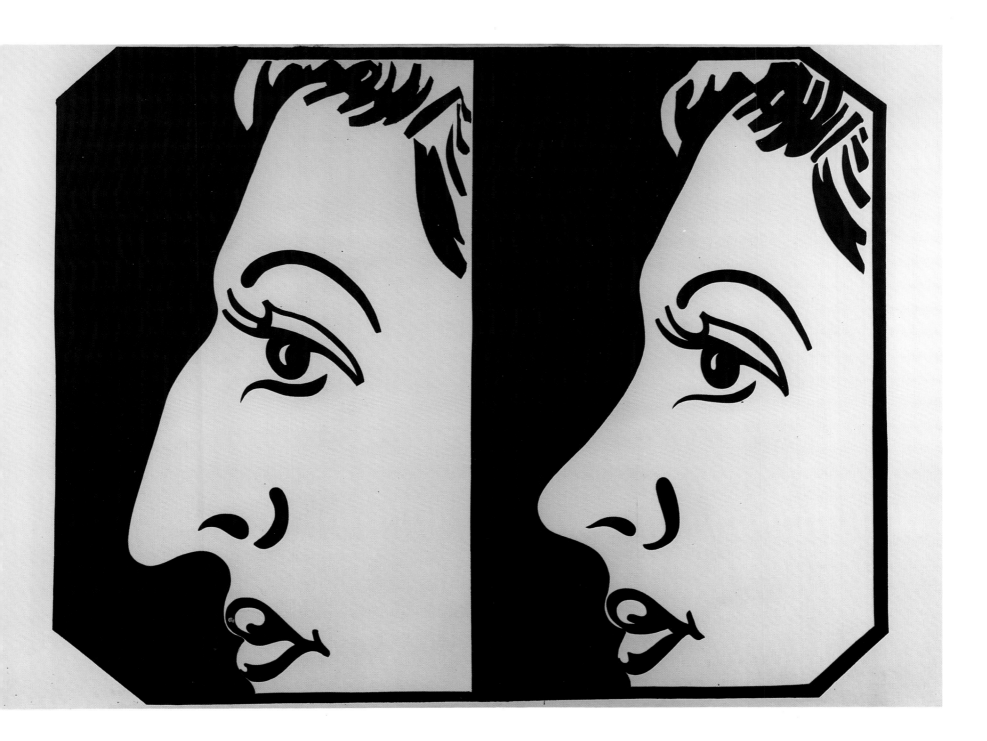

Do It Yourself (Landscape), 1962

Synthetic polymer paint and Prestype on canvas, 178 × 137 cm. Museum Ludwig, Cologne

Here again Warhol tackled the related themes of art and kitsch. Do-it-yourself or paint-by-numbers kits afford the means whereby anyone can create a passable painting by simply matching the colours in numbered tubes or pots of paint with the corresponding numbers appearing amid areas of linear drawing that are pre-printed on card, wood or canvas supports. However, in this and similar works, where commercial transfer type was employed for the numbers throughout, Warhol turned the whole do-it-yourself art concept on its head.

By inventing his own paint-by-numbers pictures, Warhol satirized cheap amateurism, the commercial and mechanistic production of 'art', and the notion of inspiration, for paint-by-numbers kits mean that anybody, however untalented, can mechanically produce a coherent picture without having to think about the process at all. And simultaneously the work also sends up the cosily familiar, if not even banal, subject-matter of do-it-yourself pictures, such as neat farmyard scenes or seascapes and beach panoramas, subjects that Warhol equally dealt with in his other *Do It Yourself* paintings. And ultimately this series of works raises highly witty but fundamental questions about art and how it is made, while simultaneously proclaiming its superiority over amateur paintings quite simply because few amateur painters using do-it-yourself kits could ever produce their pictures on the comparatively huge scale of Warhol's offerings: by blowing up such objects, the artist takes paint-by-numbers pictures out of their normal sphere and thus greatly emphasizes their fatuousness.

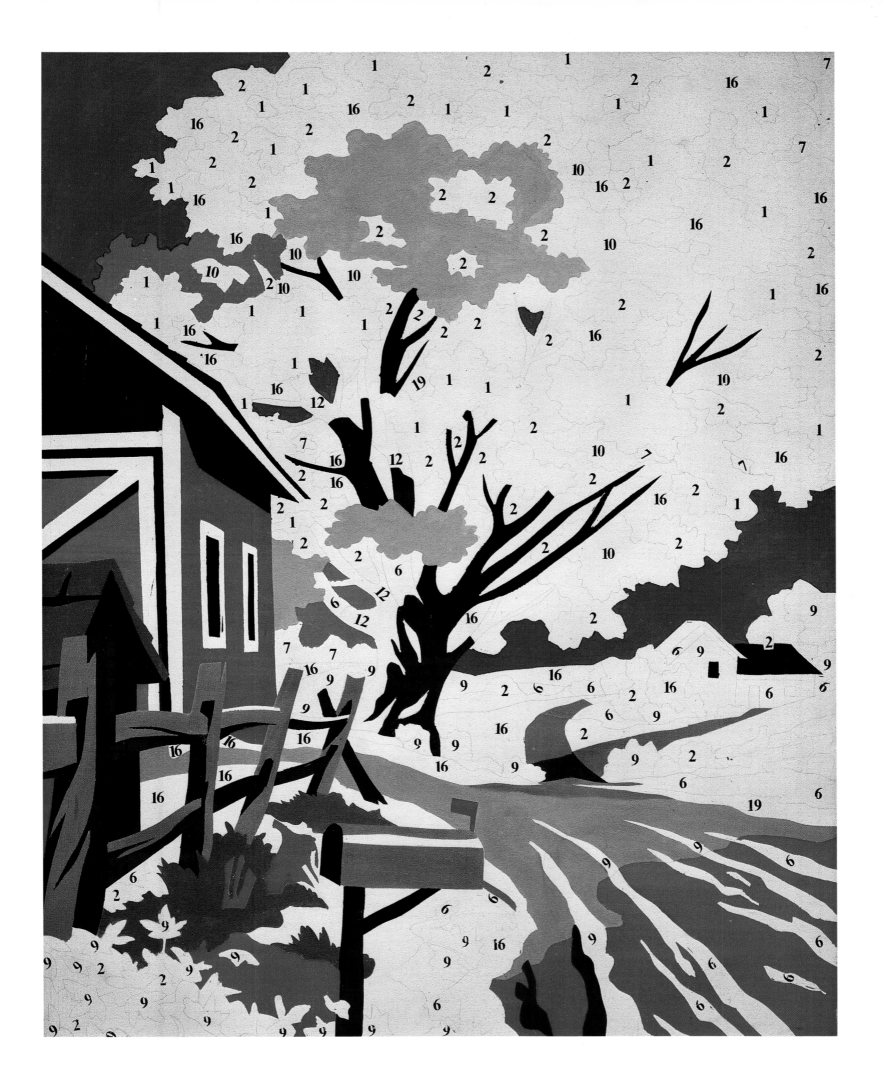

32 Soup Cans, 1961–2

Synthetic polymer paint on 32 canvases, each 50.8 × 40.6 cm. National Gallery of Art, Washington DC

This is the seminal work in Warhol's oeuvre. As narrated in the Introduction (p. 17), it was developed from an idea sold to the painter for 50 dollars by Muriel Latow in December 1961, although the visual realization of the concept was entirely Warhol's own. The group of canvases formed the artist's first one-man exhibition, held at Irving Blum's Ferus Gallery in Los Angeles in July 1962, where the works were displayed in a single line around the gallery walls, rather than in four rows of eight canvases as here. The original display maximized the repetitiousness of the imagery through being so spatially extended, and given that it filled the gallery, and that any art exhibition necessarily creates a finite world of its own, the show must therefore have ultimately projected the fearsome notion that the whole visible universe was filled with Campbell's soup.

This work was equally the first of Warhol's large-scale iconic projections. The painter developed the notion of taking an image familiar to millions and presenting it frontally, without painterly qualities, and with a flat surround (as though it were some kind of holy icon), from the *Flags* paintings of Jasper Johns which were well known to him. In the *Flags*, Johns had treated the holiest of American icons, the Stars and Stripes or 'ole glory' itself, as the starting point for a series of implied painterly and cultural questionings. However, Warhol went much further than Johns in the degree of objectivity with which he projected his icons, for by now an alliance between quasi-abstract expressionist paint-handling and popular cultural imagery in the manner of Johns no longer interested him. Instead, he isolated each of the 32 varieties of Campbell's soup so as to emphasize the sterile appearances of mechanically produced objects, and the different varieties of soup as stated on the labels force us to look hard at the images in order to perceive those slight variations, thus making us aware of how we look (or should look) closely at a work of art. And in their subject-matter these images both fly in the face of traditional notions of 'art' and simultaneously enforce the recognition that no objects are inaccessible to artistic treatment simply because they are familiar or banal: after all, if Cézanne could find apples and oranges valid artistic subjects, then why should soup-cans not equally be valid? In sum, these paintings subvert the notion of 'fine' art (a distinction that Warhol had particularly suffered from because of his previous career as a 'commercial' artist), and the very blandness of the imagery attacks artistic norms by going against the grain of the then-prevailing highly emotive surface values and serious intentions of New York school abstract art, while reminding us that blandness, like repetitiousness, underpins the consumer-orientated culture in which we live.

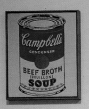
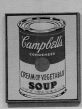
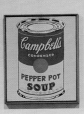
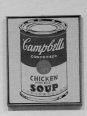
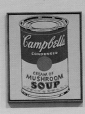
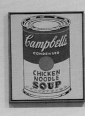
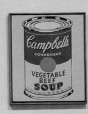
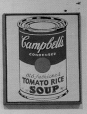
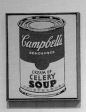
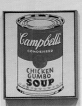
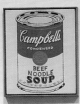
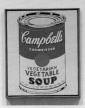
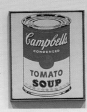
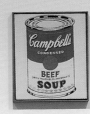
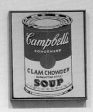
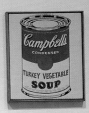
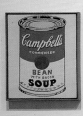
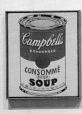
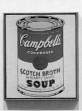

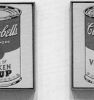
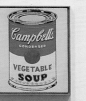
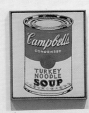
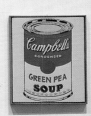
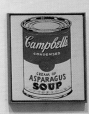
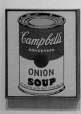
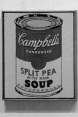
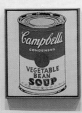
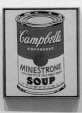
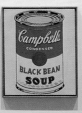
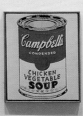
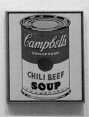
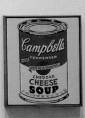

Baseball, 1962

Silkscreen ink and oil paint on canvas, 232.4 × 208.3 cm. Nelson-Atkins Museum of Art, Kansas City, Missouri

In October 1961 the baseball player Roger Maris of the New York Yankees broke Babe Ruth's home run record (which had stood since 1927) and thus was very much in the news; as well as Warhol, Robert Rauschenberg also produced a picture of Maris (*Brace*, Private Collection, USA).

This painting was exhibited in Warhol's initial New York exhibition, held in the Stable Gallery in November 1962. According to Warhol, it was the very first work in which he employed the photo-silkscreen method with which to create a multiplicity of images; previously he had relied upon hand-cut stencils and stamping devices to produce the huge replication that he saw as being essential to his art. The painter later claimed that Robert Rauschenberg had obtained the idea of using silkscreen from him but it is now impossible to establish the veracity of this claim, although *Brace* equally incorporates the photo-silkscreen method and was one of Rauschenberg's earliest paintings to do so.

From the beginning, Warhol exploited the silkscreen method to add to the associative and expressive potential of his images. As noted in the Introduction, the overlapping of the individual screened images is reminiscent of the identical effects in printer's trial proof sheets, while varieties of density in the inking impart wide-ranging rhythmic and optical dynamics to the work. At the very bottom, the increasingly over-inked obliteration of the image from left to right creates a visual intensification that was perhaps intended to parallel the impact of hitting a ball; as we shall see elsewhere, Warhol was fond of using over-inking and/or complementary colour fields to extend implied meanings in such ways.

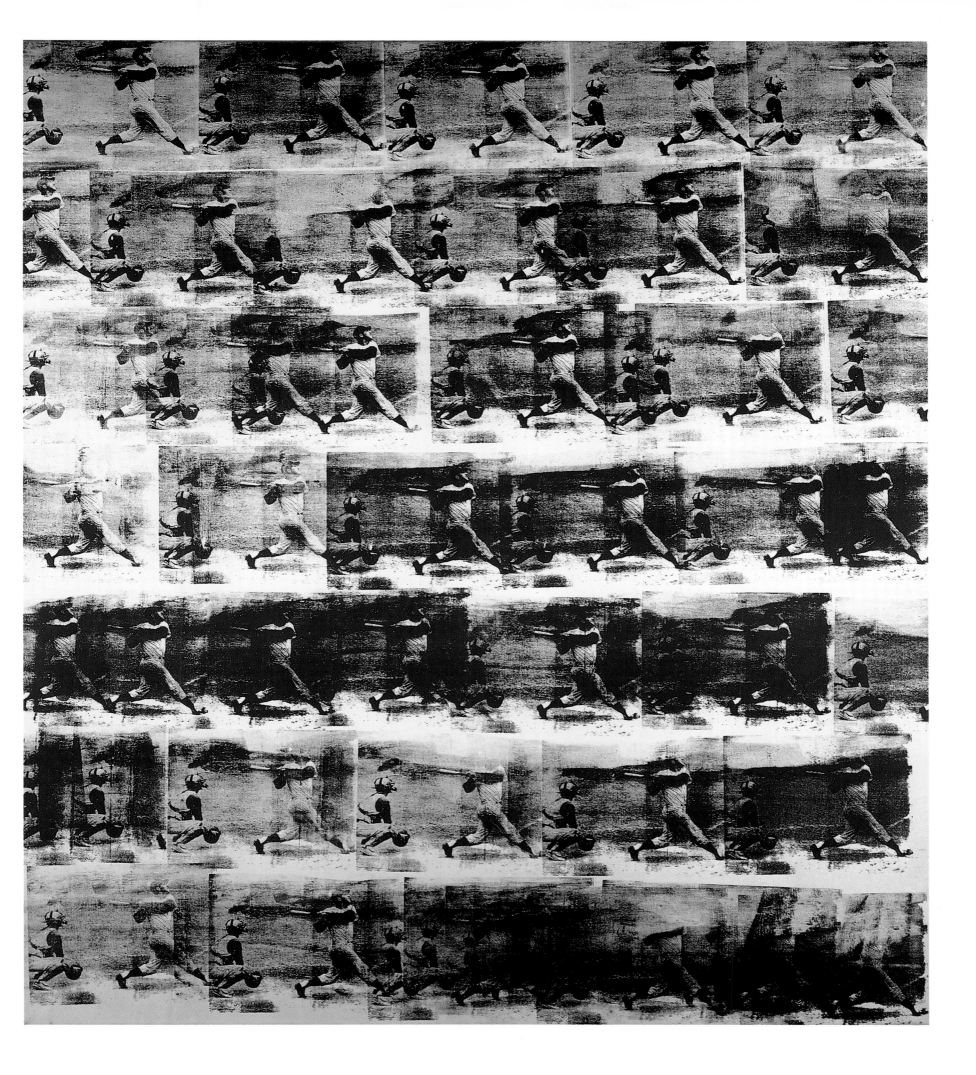

192 One-Dollar Bills, 1962

Silkscreen ink on canvas, 242 × 189 cm. Marx Collection, on loan to the Städtisches Museum Abteiberg, Mönchengladbach, Germany

As Muriel Latow also recognized in 1961, money was Warhol's very favourite subject, and he bought the idea of using it for the selfsame 50 dollars with which he purchased the Campbell's soup-cans concept from her (see Introduction, p. 16). This is one of the most visually minimalist of the many pictures of money that Warhol produced and it demonstrates exactly why the painter influenced minimalist art in the 1960s through obtaining the maximum conceptual mileage for the least visual effort. By extending all over the canvas, the dollar bills mimic the all-over visual effect of much American abstract painting, and simultaneously predicate a universe filled with money.

As there can be few people on earth who do not share Warhol's adoration of money he was certainly painting attractive subject-matter here. But equally, because these are not real money bills but artistic representations of them, he was reminding us that works of art denote monetary value, while by painting money he was cutting out the intermediate stage that other subject-matter usually represents: here we see money-as-art-as-money without the customary mask of some different subject-matter, an exact congruence indeed. The filling of every corner of the canvas with the dollar bills, and their presentation in a purely frontal manner, emphasizes their iconic nature, and thus takes further, and in a much more rigorously detached manner, the type of implied comment about idolatry that Jasper Johns had earlier made in his paintings of the American flag.

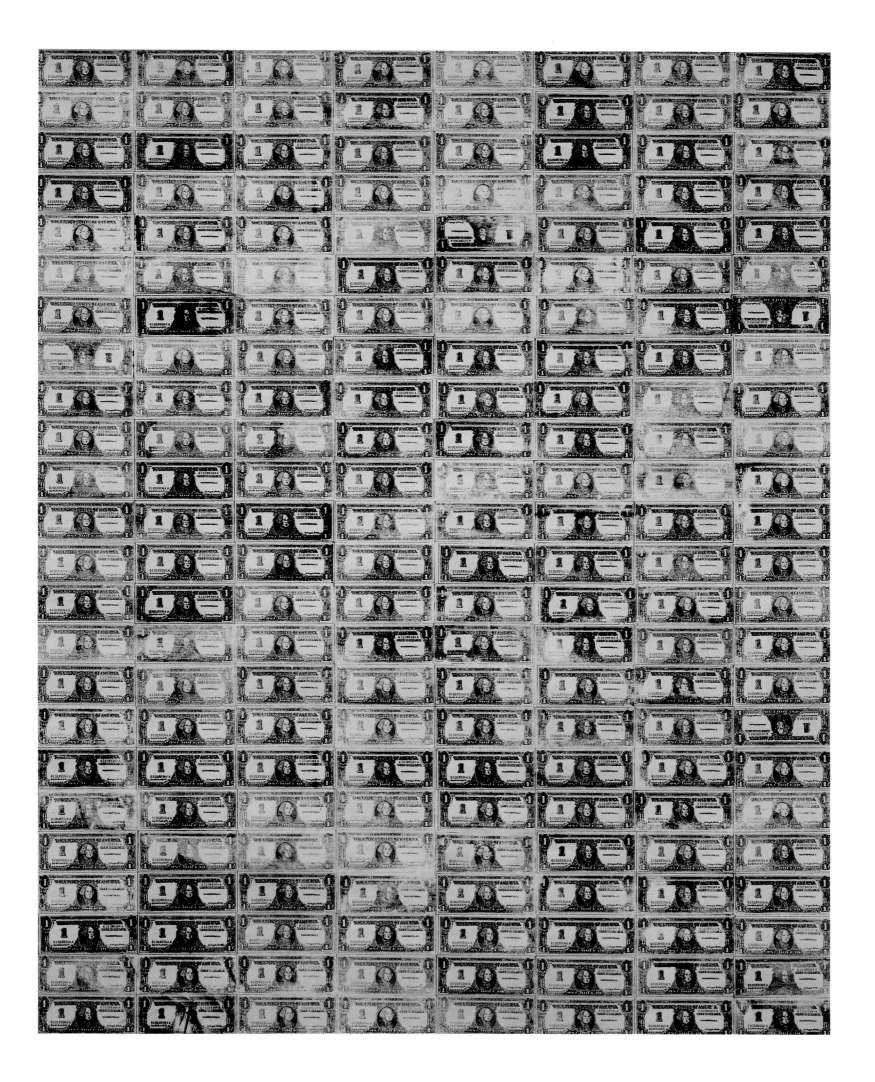

Green Coca-Cola Bottles, 1962

Silkscreen ink on synthetic polymer paint on canvas, 211 × 144.8 cm. Whitney Museum of American Art, New York

This represents yet another of the cornerstones of modern consumerism and of American culture in particular, painted iconically but entirely dispassionately and in strict ranks so as to emphasize a repetitiousness exactly mirroring the industrial process that had brought the bottles into existence in the first place. And that Warhol thought about the social implications of such imagery is made evident by his statement in *The Philosophy of Andy Warhol*, published in 1975, that

> . . . America started the tradition where the richest consumers buy essentially the same things as the poorest. You can be watching TV and see Coca-Cola, and you can know that the President drinks Coke, Liz Taylor drinks Coke, and just think, you can drink Coke, too. A Coke is a Coke and no amount of money can get you a better Coke than the one the bum on the corner is drinking. All the Cokes are the same and all the Cokes are good.

Such egalitarianism may also be expressed indirectly through the equal ranking of the bottles.

In many of Warhol's Coke bottle pictures, areas of dark colour were underpainted beneath each bottle, so as to denote the drink within, before the Coke bottle design was then overprinted in an even darker tone. Here the underpainted flat pale green areas match the colouring of empty Coke bottle glassware and they often enjoy subtle formal differences from one another that suggest various light sources for the empty bottles. Both bottles and the Coca-Cola logo were hand-drawn rather than being reproduced photographically, and the drawing of the bottle displays the type of visual shorthand that is customarily found in graphic design. Such a shorthand adds a subtle sense of personality to the imagery and offsets the effect of sterile mechanization that is induced by so much repetitiousness, just as the variations in inking bring about the same compensation whilst equally creating a subtle but necessary visual rhythm.

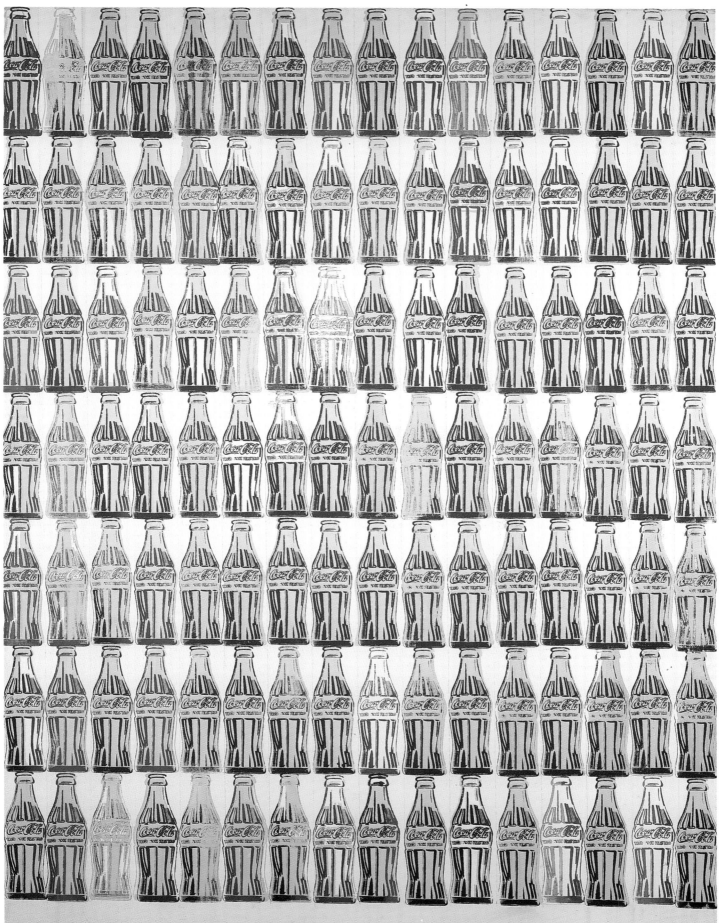

Big Torn Campbell's Soup Can, 1962

Silkscreen ink on synthetic polymer paint on canvas, 182.9 × 136 cm. Kunsthaus, Zurich

As well as painting ranks of Campbell's soup-cans and large representations of individual cans, Warhol also produced a number of pictures of damaged cans, the types of objects that are regularly thrown out by supermarkets as being unsaleable. Naturally, such 'damage' does not make Warhol's pictures of such cans unsaleable, and therein resides their irony, for whereas on the supermarket shelf most of us would undoubtedly steer clear of purchasing any can that differed from its peers, in art individuality makes wholly for attractiveness and economic value. And because damaged goods depart from a norm, ultimately these paintings of damaged soup-cans are therefore statements about individuality versus conformism which, as we have noted in the Introduction (p. 18), was a concern to Warhol in 1962.

Once again the huge enlargement of a common consumer object takes what we see far beyond the realm of realism by investing it with humour. Warhol's graphic skill is further evident in the deft visual shorthand with which the tin can is represented. In order to obtain the speckled effect on the naked part of the can, the artist mixed ordinary household washing-up detergent with his paint.

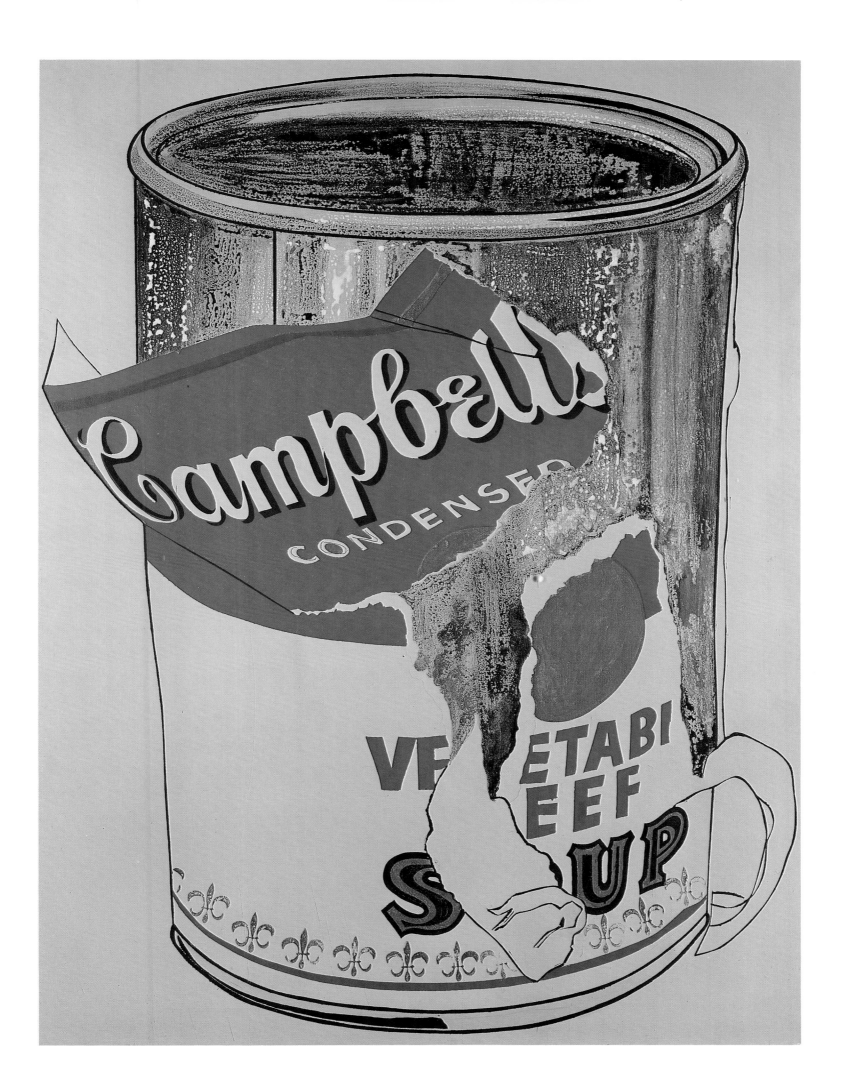

Triple Elvis, 1962

Silkscreen ink on aluminium paint on canvas, 208.3 × 152.4 cm. Virginia Museum of Fine Arts, Richmond, Virginia

We live in a culture that idolizes both consumer objects and people, and Warhol shared in this worship. Yet equally he was aware of the cultural manipulations and distortions that stimulate our regard for such idols, and he employed visual repetition to parallel those cultural processes.

Repetition forms a central physical and psychological dynamic of all industrial societies: consumer objects are mass-produced by repetitious means, their costs are minimized through standardization, and they are marketed through selling techniques that are highly repetitive. Similarly, the entertainments, leisure and advertising industries employ repetitiousness to drum home the attractiveness of their products, often by using film-stars, television personalities and the like (who are frequently themselves merchandized as commodities). And of course in terms of daily living, repetitiveness is central to all activities, from commuting to and from work, from the foods we eat to the times we eat them, in the daily or weekly timings of television and radio programmes, and in the very division between sleeping and waking time. Warhol's genius was to perceive the cultural centrality of repetitiousness and to make it the dominant subject of his art.

This image of Elvis Presley derived from a publicity still made for the 1960 film *Flaming Star*. Originally Warhol created a large number of the Elvises on a single roll of canvas which he took with him to Los Angeles in September 1963 for his second one-man show at the Ferus Gallery. On his arrival he asked the gallery director, Irving Blum, to cut the roll into conventional-format paintings mounted on wooden stretchers, and told him, 'The only thing I really want is that they should be hung edge to edge, densely – around the gallery. So long as you can manage that, do the best you can', although in the event Blum left much space around each painting. Nonetheless the hanging did look fairly dense, and it was complemented by twelve pictures of Elizabeth Taylor that were hung in an adjacent room.

According to Gerard Malanga, who was Warhol's painting assistant when the Elvises were created, it was he rather than the artist who was responsible for the overlapping multiple imaging in these paintings, saying that he 'deliberately moved the image over to create a jump effect' which Warhol liked. Again through heightening the inherent abstraction of the forms, such multiplicity forces the imagery away from merely operating on an informational level, and naturally it also calls forth associations of the repetitiousness of cinematic motion. Moreover, the aluminium-paint background looks silvery and thus introduces highly appropriate reminders of the silver screen.

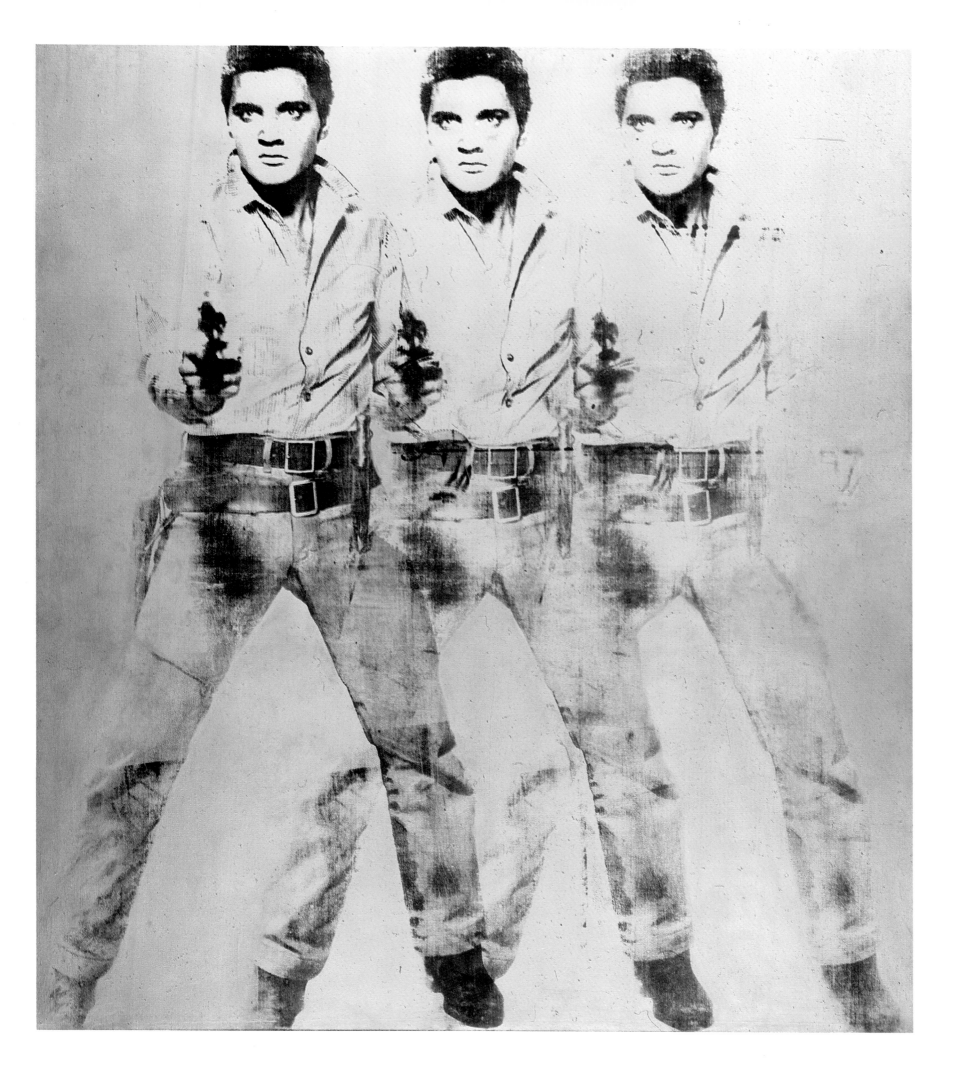

Marilyn Diptych, 1962

Silkscreen ink on synthetic polymer paint on two canvases, each 208.3 × 144.8 cm. Tate Gallery, London

Andy Warhol was prompted to embark upon his series of paintings of Marilyn Monroe by news of the actress's suicide on 4 August 1962. This is perhaps the most commemorative of all the Marilyns and it was exhibited in Warhol's New York debut exhibition in 1962.

The photograph of Marilyn Monroe that Warhol used in his paintings and prints of the actress was taken in 1953 by Gene Kornman to publicize the film *Niagara*. When producing coloured portraits such as we see partially comprising the overall work here Warhol would actually build up the picture in reverse: first he would underpaint the background and individual colour areas constituting, say, the golden hair, the pink face, the red lips, and the green eyelids and collar, before finally overprinting the silkscreened photographic image of the person being portrayed. (Sheets of transparent acetate printed with the final photographic image were temporarily laid down over the painting at each stage of its creation as an interim means of ensuring the precise alignment of the constituent elements.) The areas of garish colour are not merely visual accents but serve brilliantly to stress the garishness of Marilyn Monroe's media personality, while the slight variations in the underpaintings of the left-hand panel give variety to the 25 coloured images of Marilyn without diminishing the visual impact of the repetitiveness, with its usual implications of mass-communications media repetitiveness.

However, it is in the contrast between the cleanly painted coloured elements in the left-hand canvas and the messily painted monochromatic elements on the right that the dramatic and commemorative level to this painting clearly resides, for on the right the tonally disparate over-inking and under-inking, as well as the smeariness, introduces associations of physical obliteration and extinction that are entirely appropriate to a portrait of the dead Marilyn. By such means Warhol brilliantly juxtaposed the actress's entirely kempt and colourfully garish public personality with her psychologically messy, uncolourful and gradually disintegrating, unhappy private self.

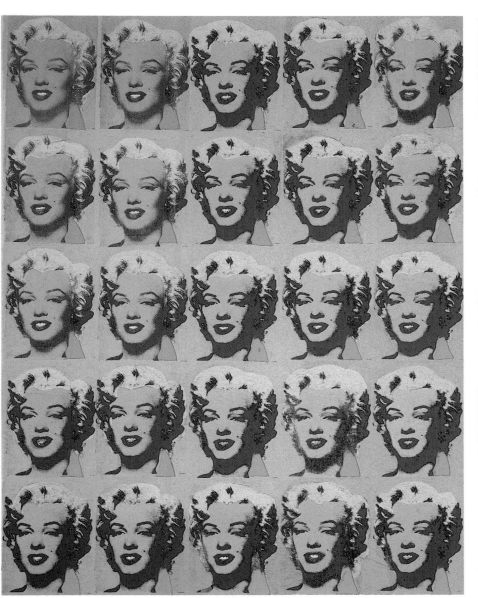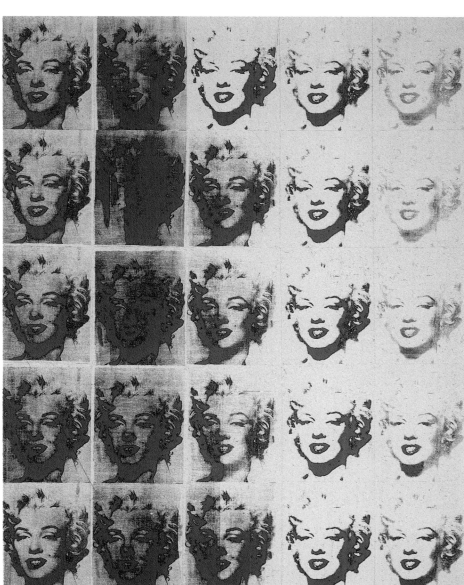

Gold Marilyn, 1962

Silkscreen ink on synthetic polymer paint on canvas, 211.4 × 144.7 cm. Museum of Modern Art, New York

If in recent times Marilyn Monroe was perhaps the supreme symbol of Western male notions of womanhood and sexuality, then Andy Warhol's *Gold Marilyn* is surely the supreme artistic icon of that mythicality, for because of its golden background, this picture comes closer to looking like a religious icon than most of the painter's other iconic images. Ultimately Warhol developed the work from the Flags paintings of Jasper Johns, although that does not in any way detract from his achievement in engaging a rather different set of ideas and associations in the work.

There is another of the paintings shown in Warhol's first New York exhibition in 1962. Some of the major components of Marilyn's glamour – her peroxide hairdo, eyelids and lips, as well as her basic facial skin area and shirt-collar – are luridly heightened in colour so as to stress the garishness of glamour. And the surrounding of the actress's head by a vast sea of gold paint introduces unmistakeable associations of wealth and economic value, thus reminding us that Marilyn Monroe was at the cutting edge of a vast and highly exploitative financial operation, as are all successful media superstars.

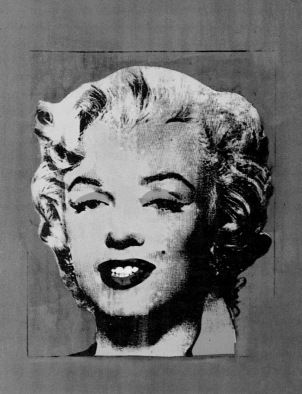

Marilyn Monroe's Lips, 1962

Silkscreen ink on synthetic polymer paint and pencil on two canvases, 210.2 × 205.1 and 211.8 × 210.8 cm. Hirshhorn Museum and Sculpture Garden, Smithsonian Institution, Washington DC

This is perhaps Warhol's wittiest work, and ultimately it may have derived from the sofa that Salvador Dalí created of Mae West's lips around 1936, although the repetitiousness makes these lips into something very different.

In the public appreciation of any glamorous mass-media personality, the isolation of certain physiognomical and anatomical details – eyes, lips, breasts, buttocks, legs – plays an important psycho-sexual role, and by filling this work entirely with the isolated detail of Marilyn's mouth, Warhol not only stressed such psycho-sexual detailing but also turned a physiognomical feature that was very glamorous in the full context of the face into something rather repulsive. This linkage of glamour and ugliness would recur in Warhol's work, as we shall see. The endless repetitiveness makes Warhol's customary point about mass-communications media repetitiousness, whilst simultaneously pushing the imagery to the verge of total abstraction, thus enforcing a link with the typical pictorial rhythms of contemporary 'all-over' abstract paintings and perhaps even satirizing the formal monotony of many such works, something that Warhol was possibly to do again later but on a much vaster scale in the *Shadows* series of paintings of the late 1970s.

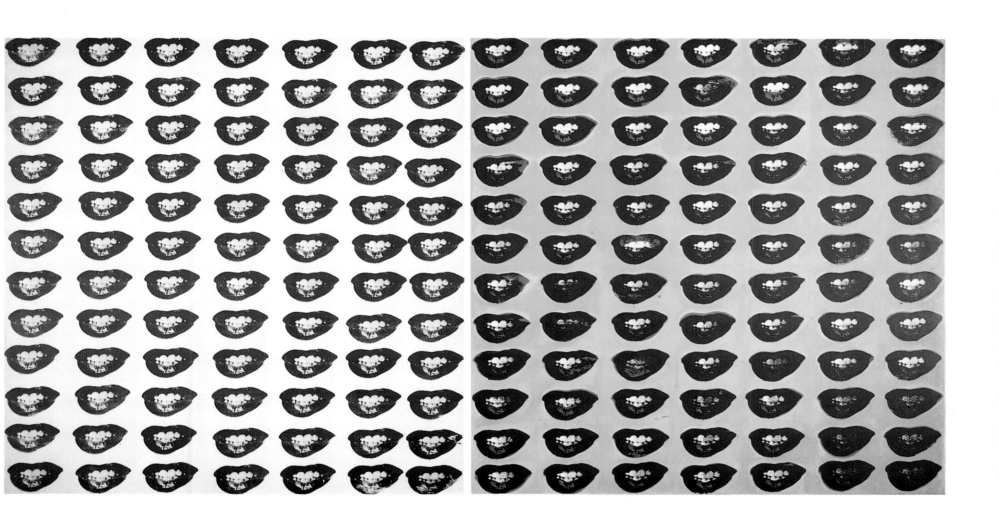

Red Race Riot, 1963

Silkscreen ink on synthetic polymer paint on canvas, 350 × 210 cm. Museum Ludwig, Cologne

Although Warhol's attention was drawn to the ugly side of American life in 1962, when he painted *149 Die in Jet* (see Introduction, p. 20), it was not until the following year – by which time he had mastered silkscreen printing and painting techniques – that he really began to grapple with tragic subject-matter, firstly in a group of Race Riot images and then in further pictures of commotion, disaster and death.

For this painting Warhol used three photographs of police dogs being unleashed on civil rights protesters in Birmingham, Alabama, pictures by Charles Moore that had originally appeared in the 17 May 1963 edition of *Life* magazine. Warhol was never politically committed, so it would be wrong to see here any particular position regarding the Civil Rights struggle, but nonetheless the imagery does speak frighteningly for itself. Warhol's arrangement of the component images forces us to look carefully in order to distinguish one photo from another, and the internal diagonals enforced by legs, batons, dogs and torn trousers create a number of powerful linear cross-rhythms that offset the rectilinearity of the individual images. The graininess of the photos is counterpoised by the smeariness of the background colour, thus further pushing the imagery towards abstraction, and that very smeariness, plus its colour, introduces appropriate associations of blood.

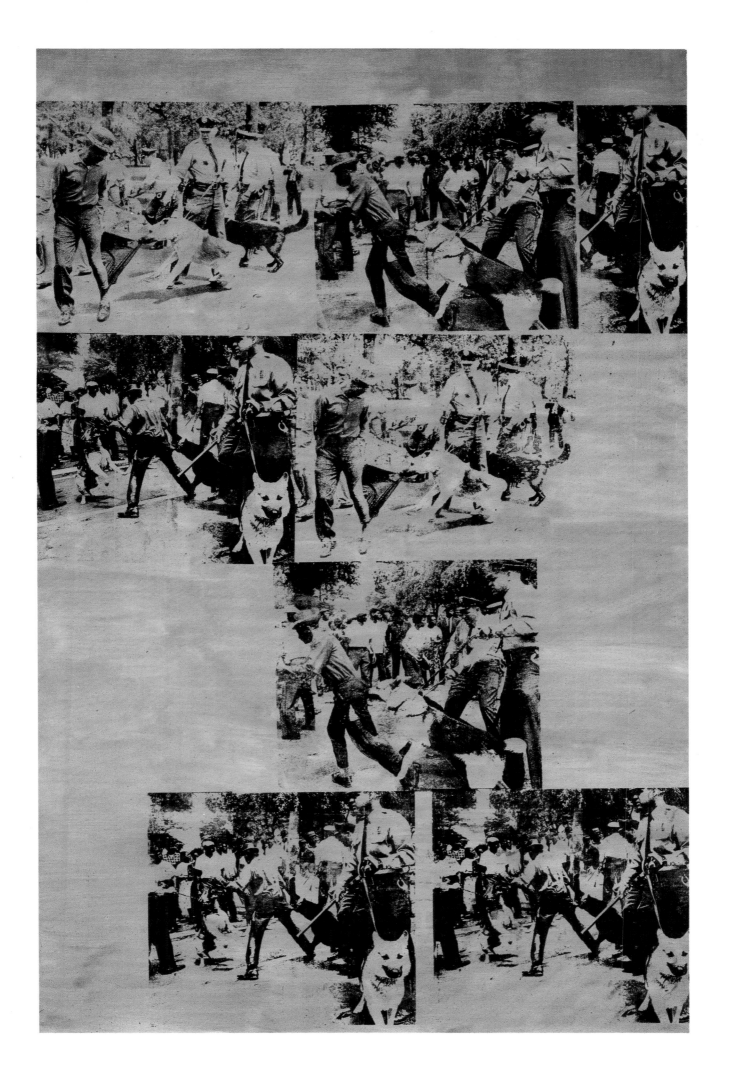

Suicide, 1963

Silkscreen ink on synthetic polymer paint on canvas, 313 × 211 cm. Kunstsammlung Nordrhein-Westfalen, Düsseldorf, Germany

When it comes to death and disaster most of us are voyeurs: bad news sells newspapers or forces us repeatedly to our television sets and radios, and very few of us are not intrigued by mass disasters. Certainly such matters were frequently dealt with in post-Renaissance art, as in the hordes of pictures of shipwrecks, avalanches, volcanic eruptions, murders by *banditti* and other natural or man-made catastrophes, as well as being articulated more recently in horror fiction and movies. Perhaps this attraction has its roots in the reminder that 'there, but for the grace of God, go I', but it is a morbid form of escapism nonetheless. Yet Warhol's Death and Disaster pictures subtly differ from all their predecessors, for there is not a trace of pleasurable morbidity here: the painter simply confronts us with the fact of death dispassionately and with a heightened sense of emotional and pictorial abstraction (the one informing the other), as if to ask, 'here is the clinical reality of death – what are you looking at, are you deriving pleasure from it, and if so, why?'

Through Warhol's purposeful indifference to precise matchings of tone and form, the variations and overlappings of inking in this image boost both the sense of movement of the falling suicide and the feeling of impersonality that the picture projects. Moreover, the tonal variety augments the inherent pictorial abstraction, but again that forces us to question how we can concern ourselves with such aesthetic matters when confronted by the death of others: surely some subject-matter is located beyond the reach of art, and thus the aesthetic pleasures it affords? And naturally the repetition of the images reinforces our awareness of how repetitiveness is constantly employed to communicate tragedy in the world around us.

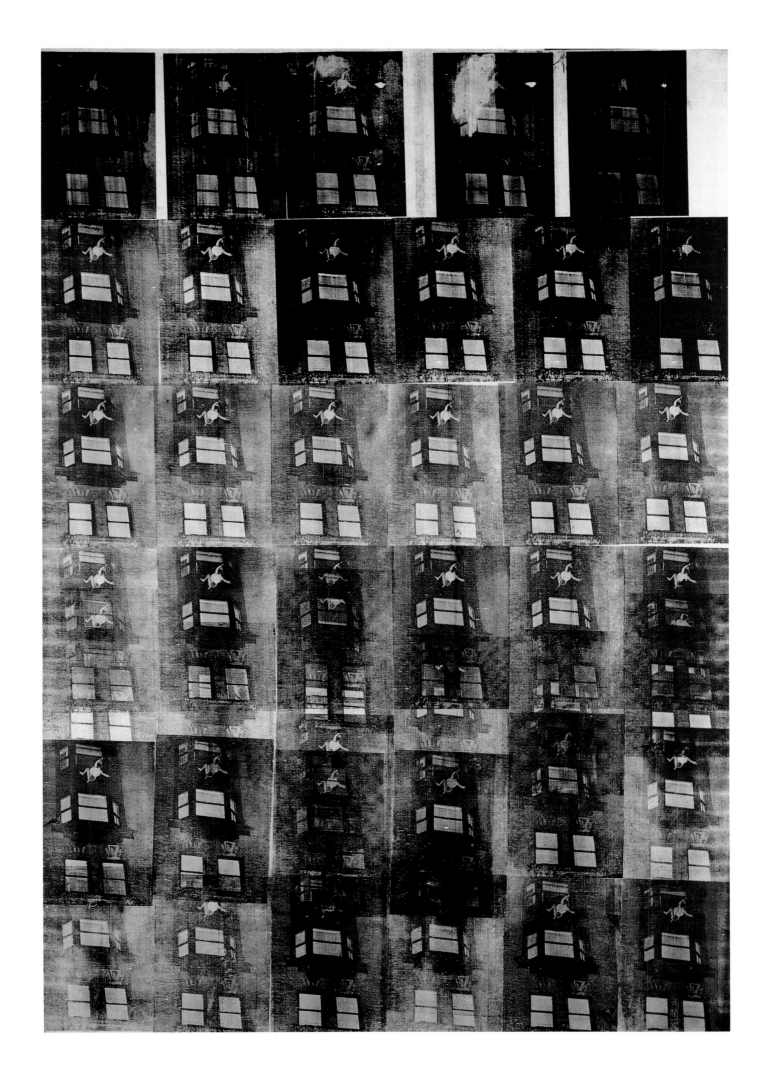

Tunafish Disaster, 1963

Silkscreen ink on synthetic polymer paint on canvas, 316 × 211 cm. Saatchi Collection, London

There is a pair of *Tunafish Disaster* paintings, and in both works Warhol subtly combined the statement about deviation from a norm that he had earlier made in his Damaged Soup-Can pictures, with his current preoccupation with death and disaster, for of course the tins of A & P Chunk Light Tuna that gave these two Detroit housewives botulism and thus killed them would not have differed outwardly on the supermarket shelf from identical cans of untainted fish. The visual repetitions and juxtapositions emulate printer's rough proof sheets, and the smudginess further heightens the immediacy of the imagery through bringing into play associations with newspaper printing. And as always with Warhol's disaster pictures, we are forced to question our reasons for wanting to look at these unfortunate women in the first place.

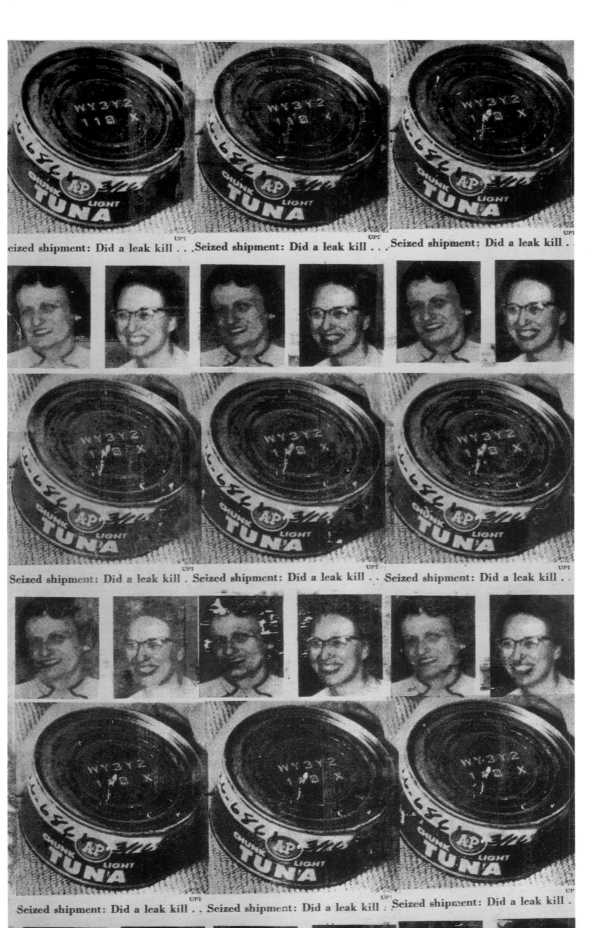

Seized shipment: Did a leak kill . . . Seized shipment: Did a leak kill . . . Seized shipment: Did a leak kill . . .

Seized shipment: Did a leak kill . Seized shipment: Did a leak kill . . Seized shipment: Did a leak kill .

Seized shipment: Did a leak kill . . Seized shipment: Did a leak kill . Seized shipment: Did a leak kill .

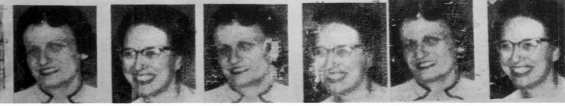

Five Deaths Seventeen Times in Black and White, 1963

Silkscreen ink on synthetic polymer paint on canvas, two canvases, each 262 × 209 cm. Oeffentliche Kunstsammlung, Kunstmuseum, Basle

Warhol may have first obtained the idea of specifically dealing with smashed cars from the sculpture entitled *Jackpot* by the American sculptor John Chamberlain that he owned, a piece that he bought in 1961 and which comprises the crushed body of an automobile painted in factory colours. But certainly because of that work he cannot have been unaware of the physical damage wrought by smashing a car body. The painter gleaned the photographs he used for the car-crash pictures from police and press files that respectively were not released for use to the press or were unpublishable, being deemed too horrific.

Through its monochromatic starkness, this is one of the most visually powerful of all of Warhol's car-crash disaster pictures. Yet again visual repetitiousness confuses the eye to augment the inherent abstraction contained in the imagery, and equally that repetitiveness reminds us that death is everywhere, while the uneven inking enforces subtle differences between the individual images, thus lending visual variety to the work. But ultimately the imaginative power of this picture resides in the relationship between its two distinct halves.

Warhol attached an identically-sized but wholly blank canvas to many of the paintings he produced during the early 1960s and he made a number of different claims for having done so. One was that the coupling gave purchasers twice as much art for their money; another was that conversely they were paying good money for empty canvases. A further reason had to do with Warhol's admiration for the flat-patterned, abstract paintings of Ellsworth Kelly (one of which he owned), for as he stated, 'I always liked Ellsworth's work, and that's why I always painted a blank canvas.' But in addition to these stated aims, it also seems possible that the blank canvases were intended to heighten the meaning of the pictures they complemented.

Blankness is not necessarily without meaning, for it can easily signify absence. Thus in the paired disaster paintings the vast, complementary flat areas of colour or blank tone heighten the sense that the horrific events represented nearby are being met with emptiness, and in the light of Warhol's stated emotional neutrality and *anomie*, that blankness could well have been intended to stand for something larger, namely a cosmic emptiness or indifference. And in the present work the blankness and utter blackness of the right-hand canvas certainly does project the finality and endless blackness of annihilation, as experienced by the deceased victims of the crash on the left.

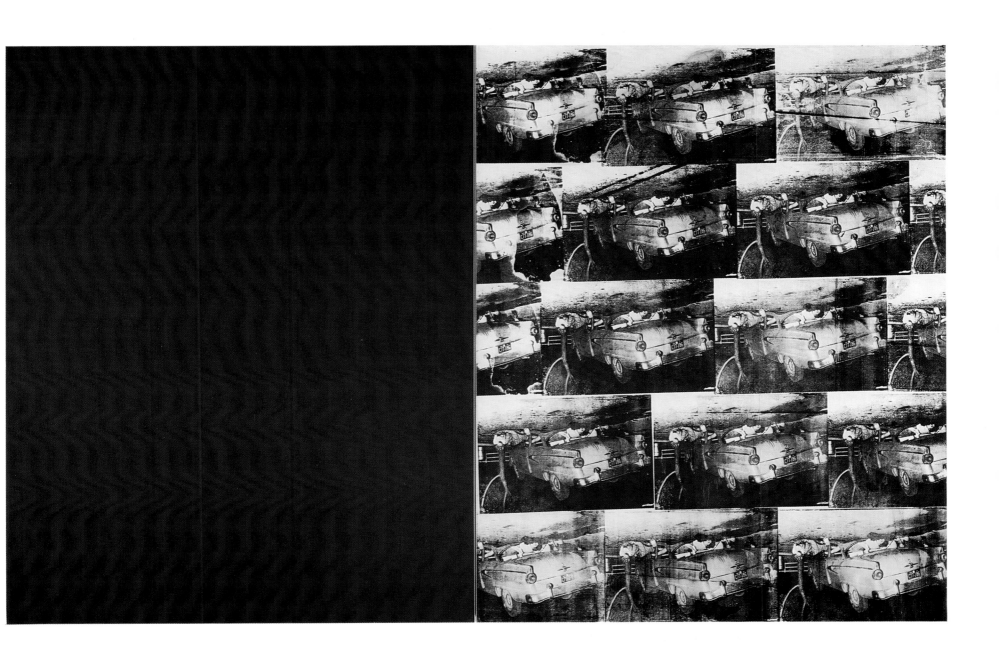

Orange Car Crash Ten Times, 1963

Silkscreen ink on synthetic polymer paint on canvas, 269.2 × 208.2 cm. Museum Ludwig, Cologne, Germany

The garishness of the opposed orange background and overprinted maroon colour of the car-crash imagery here creates an intense visual stridency that parallels the tortured physical dynamics of the car crash, and the abstract patternings of the repetitious images not only force us to look hard at the work so as to apprehend exactly what we are seeing, but they also underline the irony that in carefully examining them we are playing down tragedy in pursuit of a perceptual, if not even an aesthetic experience. The seemingly random, off-centre placing of the tragic images projects a more universal arbitrariness, whilst the overwhelming blankness of surrounding and complementary colour areas once again heightens our sense of the ultimately cosmic meaninglessness of the tragedy that is set before us. It is with images like these that Julian Schnabel's claim that Warhol 'presented the horror of our time with the thoroughness of Goya in his time' seems most borne out.

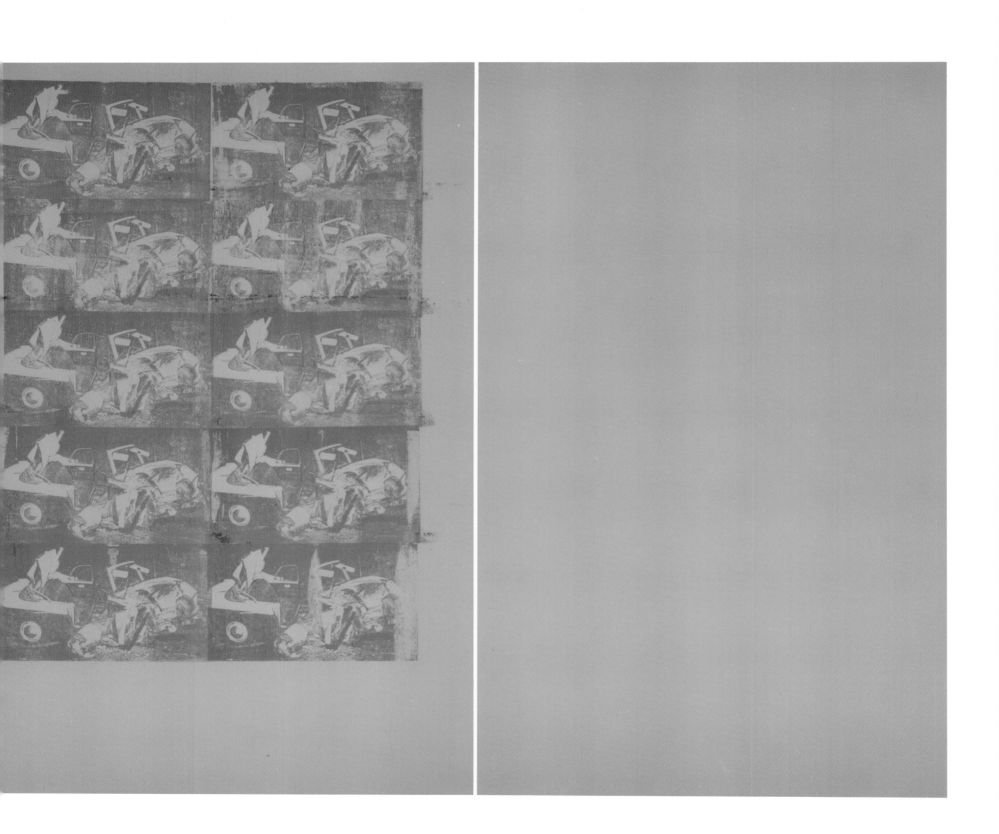

Optical Car Crash, 1962

Silkscreen ink on synthetic polymer paint on canvas, 208 × 208.3 cm. Oeffentliche Kunstsammlung, Kunstmuseum, Basle

Here Warhol's tendency to push his imagery towards abstraction took over almost completely, with the painting walking a fine line between representationalism and the type of investigation into the perceptual qualities of paintings that was being explored contemporaneously in the early 1960s by Op Artists. Yet simultaneously the massive overlaps and blurred inkings, and the vibrancy of the strident green and hot orange colours, enforce a wholly appropriate dramatic level to the work, for of course the visual confusions and clashings of form parallel the confusions and clashings of the crashed vehicles, whilst the sharply contrasting colours certainly project the dynamic physical tensions of their impact.

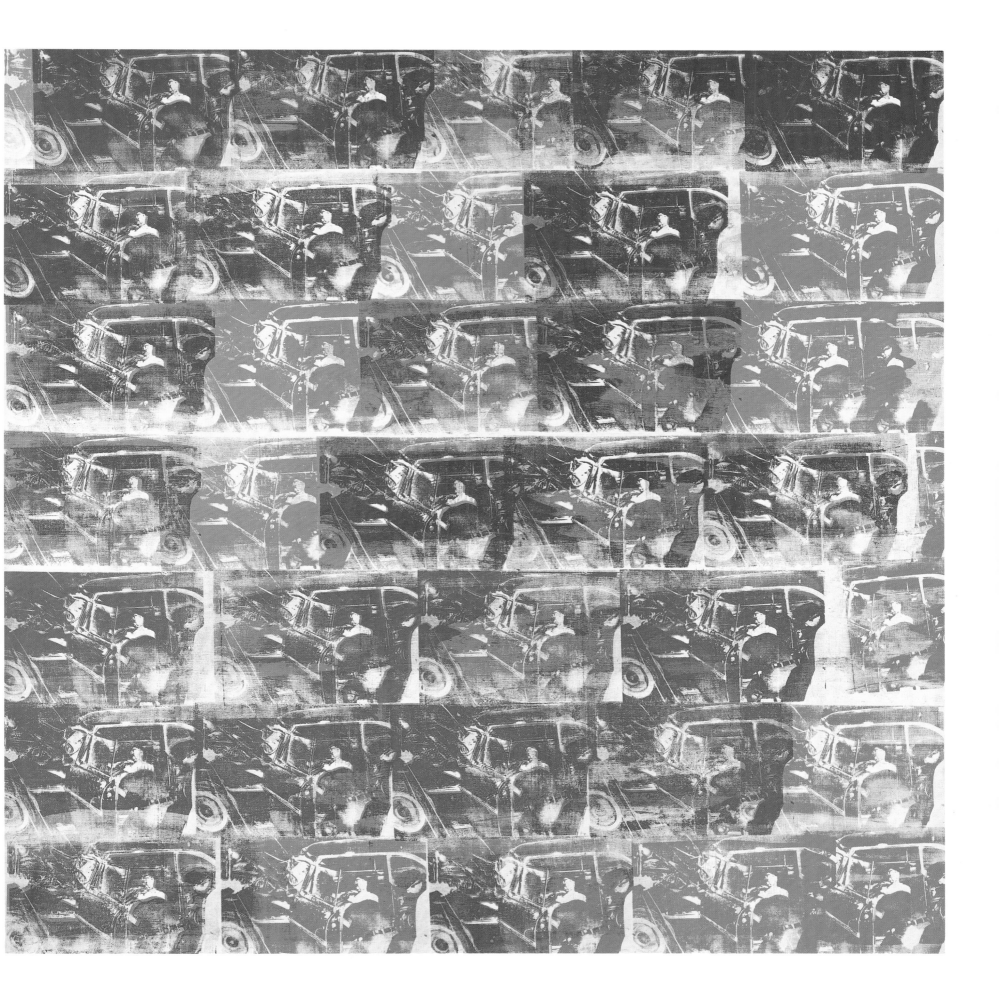

Ethel Scull 36 Times, 1963

Silkscreen ink on synthetic polymer paint on 36 canvases, 202.6 × 363.2 cm overall. Whitney Museum of American Art, New York

This was Warhol's first commissioned silkscreen portrait, and it was ordered and paid for by Robert Scull, the New York taxi-fleet owner who was amongst the most prominent collectors of new art in the early 1960s.

Warhol's customary habit of directly confronting reality paid off brilliantly here. Knowing that the painter wanted to use photographs of her for the portrait, Ethel Scull imagined that he would get someone like Richard Avedon to take the pictures, and accordingly she dolled herself up in an Yves St Laurent suit for the photographic session. However, Warhol instead took her to a group of 42nd Street photo-booth machines that he fed with small change; as the sitter later told Emile de Antonio:

> He said, 'Just watch the red light,' and I froze. I watched the red light and never did anything. So Andy would come in and poke me and make me do all kinds of things, and I relaxed finally. I think the whole place . . . thought they had two nuts there. We were running from one booth to another, and he took all these pictures, and they were drying all over the place.

Warhol then selected 17 of the photographs for the portrait, some of which appear several times, and photo-silkscreened them on individual panels before finally having them assembled in the Sculls' Fifth Avenue apartment to form one work.

The novel result of Warhol's approach was that in effect Ethel Scull portrayed herself here, for by posing both self-consciously and unselfconsciously, she thus revealed facets of her personality that would normally be hidden by more conventional portrait methods. She herself liked the work, for as she told Emile de Antonio, '. . . it was a portrait of being alive and not like those candy box things, which I detest, and never ever wanted as a portrait of myself'.

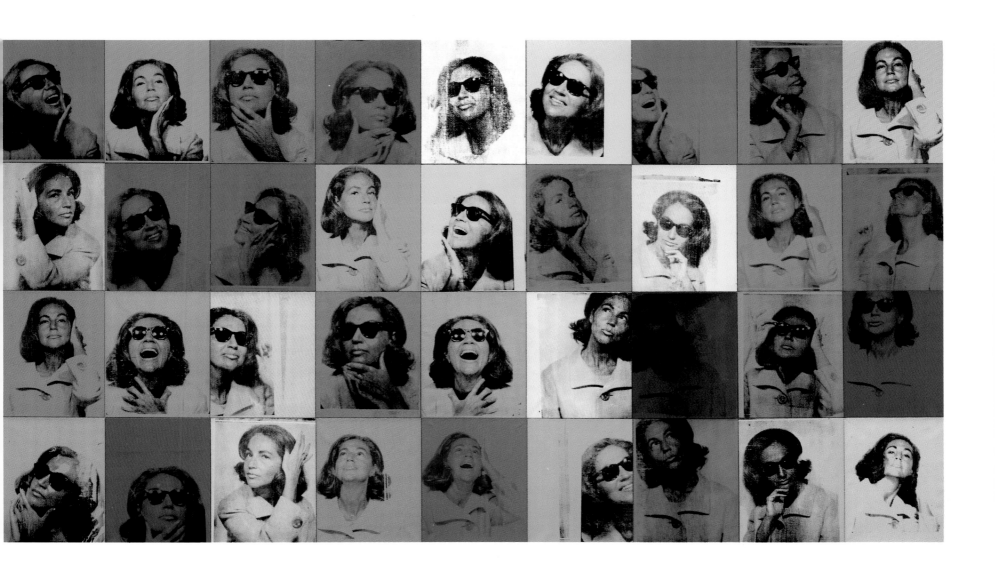

Mona Lisa, 1963

Silkscreen ink on synthetic polymer paint on canvas, 319.4 × 208.6 cm. Blum Helman Gallery, New York

The *Mona Lisa* is without doubt the most famous artistic icon in the world, and it has thus long been a potent symbol for those who wish to attack the traditional cultural values it represents. Perhaps the best-known such attack is Marcel Duchamp's *L.H.O.O.Q.* of 1919 in which a moustache and goatee were pencilled on a reproduction of the *Mona Lisa*, with a ribald, phonetically punning abbreviation added below, a work that Warhol probably knew.

As narrated in the Introduction (p. 23), the Leonardo was lent to the Metropolitan Museum of Art, New York, in February 1963 for a month, and the tremendous media hullabaloo it caused motivated Warhol to produce a number of large-scale paintings which recycle the image. As a means of mirroring the endlessly repetitive cultural treatment that was being meted out to the *Mona Lisa*, Warhol emphasized replication in these works and he even entitled one of them *Thirty Are Better Than One* (Private Collection), a wry comment on the popular equation of value with multiplicity. In the version reproduced here, however, Warhol dealt instead with the reproduction of a work of art by the print media, and specifically by colour printing.

Colour reproductions break images down into three colours: cyan (a sharp sky blue), magenta (a deep red) and yellow, plus black and white, from the combinations of which all other colours and tones are obtained. It is exactly those three colours and two tones that Warhol has employed here. Moreover, the imagery of this painting relates even more specifically to the processes of commercial colour printing, by which reproductions of the *Mona Lisa* are churned out in their millions, for it makes the overall image look exactly like a colour printer's rough proof sheet, with seemingly arbitrary overprintings of the type that come about when colour printers run off preliminary colour proofs and do not want to use up endless sheets of paper whilst doing so – usually they will just overprint on a single sheet of paper. And that is exactly what Warhol has duplicated here, for he must have seen such rough proofs many times during his commercial art career. Near the top right a slight misregistration of the cyan and magenta printings is wittily emulated, but otherwise the head or hands of the *Mona Lisa* remain perfectly legible, although such clarity does nothing to compromise the overall sense that this picture is made up of arbitrary overprintings.

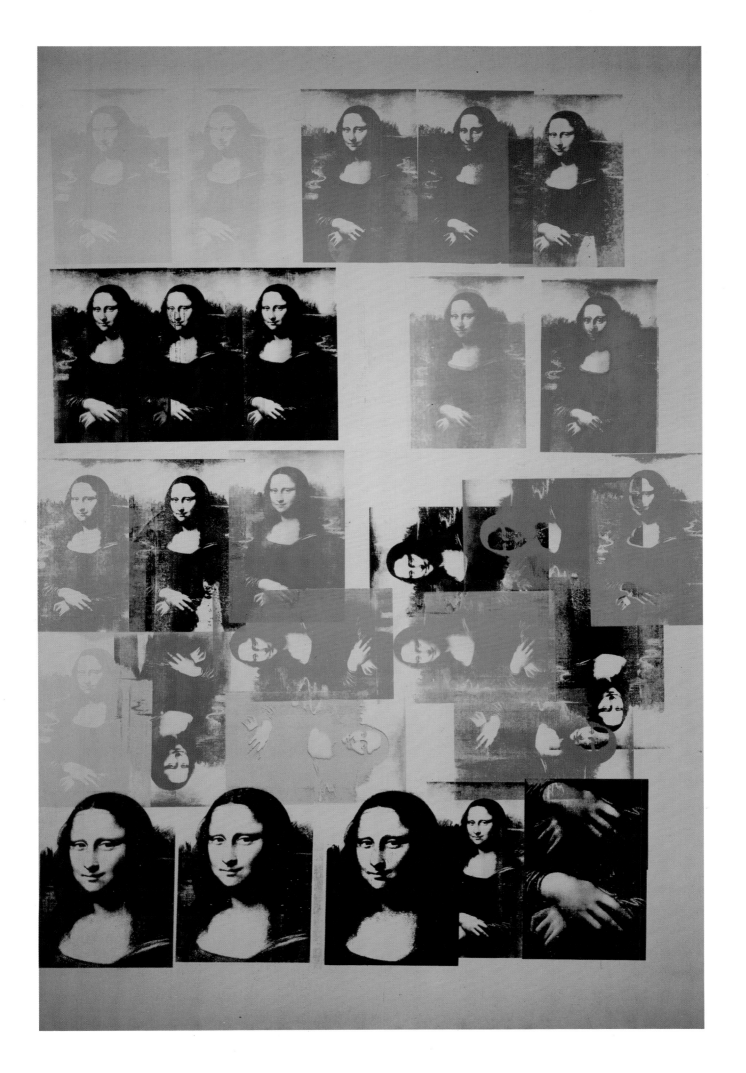

Blue Electric Chair, 1963

Silkscreen ink on synthetic polymer paint on two canvases, each 266.7 × 203.8 cm. Saatchi Collection, London

Death by electrocution was widely debated in New York State in 1963, being used for the last two times in Sing Sing prison in March and August of that year. Warhol produced a large number of images of the electric chair, but he did not rely merely upon the inherent emotive associations of the object depicted to convey the horror of what it stands for. Instead, in some of the Electric Chairs he superimposed the silkscreened image of the chairs in black ink over areas of attractive colour and thus enforced the ironic juxtaposition of horror and prettiness, a linkage that he may have seen as a metaphor for life itself, while in others of the works he overprinted the chairs in extremely polarized colours that carry unmistakeable associations of the way that photographic sensitivities are affected by high-energy electrical discharges. Such a metaphorical colouring encourages one to interpret the vivid blue colour of this work as similarly denoting something beyond the visible, namely a powerful electrical voltage, just as the repetitiousness of the electric chair image may have been intended to remind us of the long series of executions that the chair had effected. And certainly the emptiness of the right-hand panel conveys a blankness that may be interpreted as signifying the emptiness of death itself.

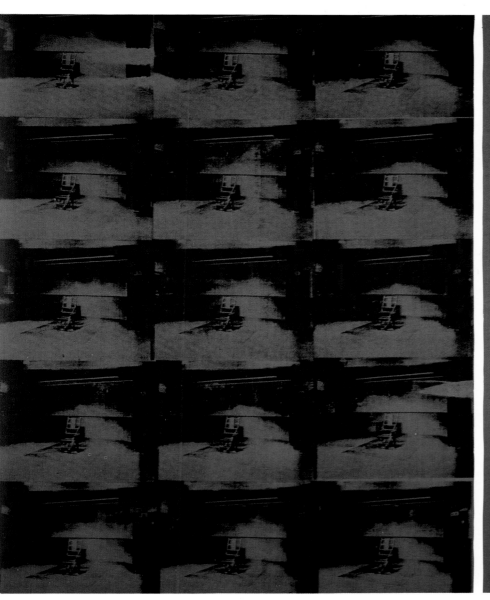 

Atomic Bomb, c. 1963

Silkscreen ink on synthetic polymer paint on canvas, 264.1 × 204.5 cm. Saatchi Collection, London

This painting has usually been dated to 1965, but it seems likely that it dates from earlier. As Warhol's birthday was on 6 August, he had every reason to be aware of atomic explosions, for it was on his seventeenth birthday in 1945 that the first atomic bomb was dropped on Hiroshima.

Despite Warhol's disclaimers to have expressed any meanings in his works, this painting indubitably demonstrates that he *did* employ his imagery to say something about the world, for the red colour (which bears connotations of fire) and the gradual blackening of the image so that it totally clogs the grid-sectors of the work towards the bottom right-hand corner, create a brilliant metaphor for the utter annihilation that is quickly brought about by an atomic explosion.

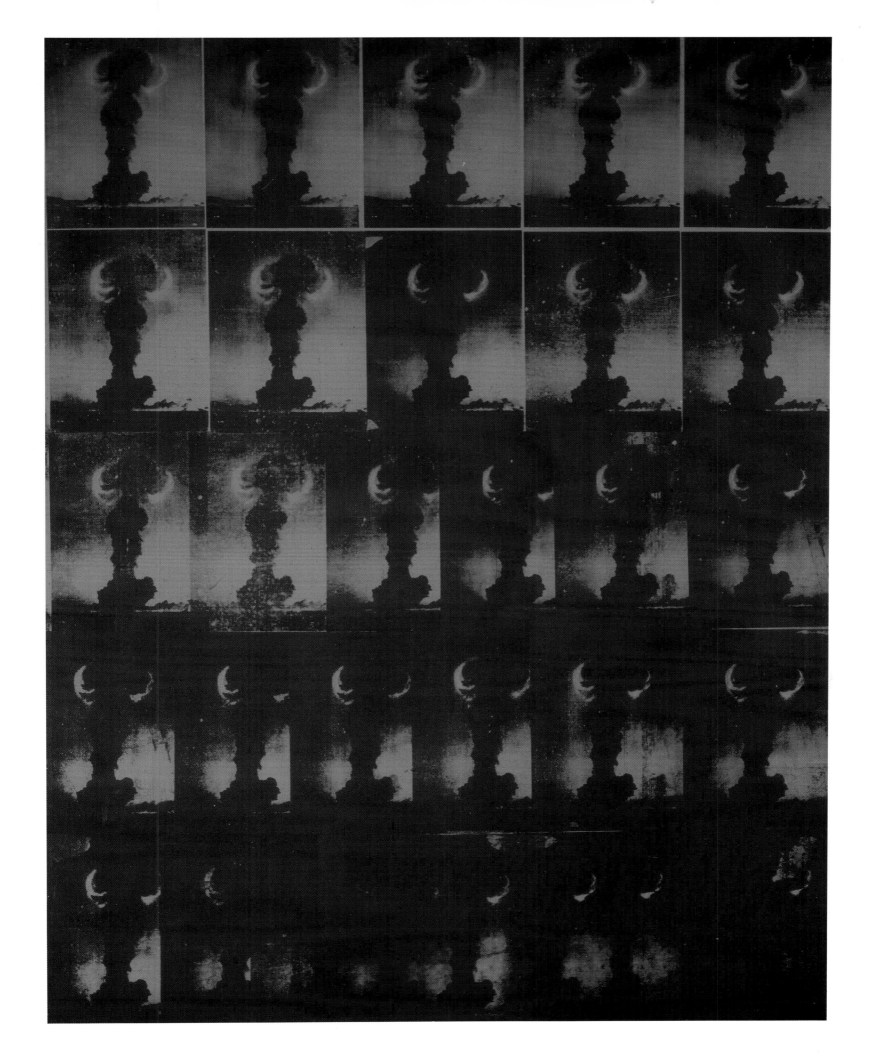

Elvis I and II, 1964

Silkscreen ink on synthetic polymer paint on canvas, two canvases, each 208.3 cm square. Art Gallery of Ontario, Toronto

Not the least of Warhol's talents was his ability to select images judiciously, and through using a publicity photo of Elvis Presley as a cowboy pointing a gun, the painter both appropriated a major American area of myth into his art and touched upon the violence that stands at the very heart of that myth. Yet in its coloured form the image does triple duty, for through the garish simplification of the colour it projects cultural banality, which is highly appropriate, as Elvis Presley looks extremely kitsch as a cowboy.

The images on the right are silkscreened over aluminium paint and that underlying metallic sheen introduces unmistakeable associations of the silver screen, while the cloning of the images equally projects the cloning of cultural images by the mass media. Towards the right the tonality lightens, which may have been accidental but which nonetheless could be interpreted as implying that even superstars fade.

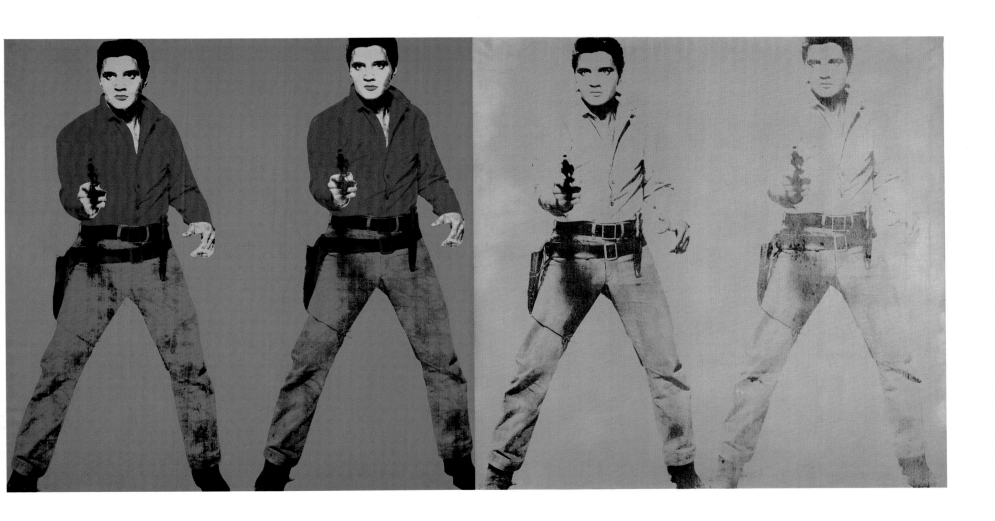

The American Man – Watson Powell, 1964

Silkscreen ink on synthetic polymer paint on canvas, 326.4 × 163.8 cm. American Republic Insurance Company, Des Moines, Iowa, USA

It seems apt that just as Warhol dealt with almost every other aspect of contemporary life in his art, so too he should have created the archetypal businessman's portrait, bland but multitudinous. This portrait was commissioned by the insurance company that still owns it, and it represents the then-President of the organization. The photograph of Watson Powell that Warhol used was one frequently handed out by the company, so the replication of the image was therefore extremely apt. Warhol gave the work its present title, presumably because he saw Watson Powell as the archetypal American male, although in private he always referred to him as 'Mr Nobody'.

The English painter and art critic Mark Lancaster visited Warhol when he was mixing and testing the colours for the portrait, and the latter complained of having to do such work instead of making movies. Yet Lancaster gained the impression 'that [Warhol] was absorbed and happy in this activity'. The varied tones of beige, white and black create a subtle visual rhythm and offset the repetitiousness of the imagery, while the colours themselves effectively project the requisite emotional neutrality of an official, corporate image.

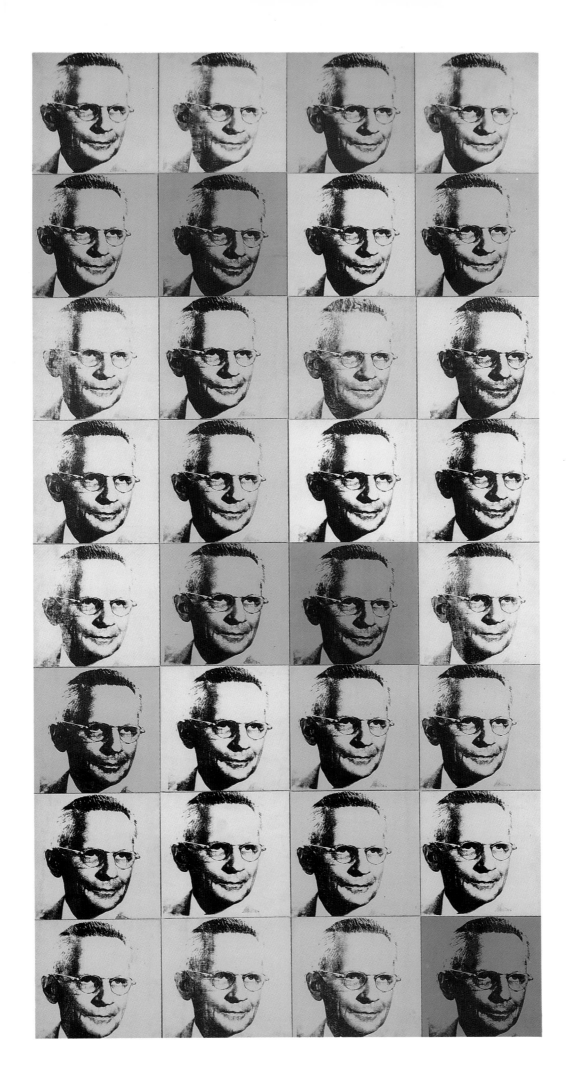

Most Wanted Men, 1964

In April 1964 Warhol was invited by the architect Philip Johnson to adorn the outside of the New York State Pavilion at the New York World's Fair, and initially he planned to make a work using Heinz brand pickles in order to allude to the pickles that had been handed out at the previous New York World's Fair in 1939. Yet, perhaps because he remembered a poster by Marcel Duchamp that he had seen in Los Angeles the previous year, he soon changed tack. (The Duchamp poster reproduced one of the French artist's works dating from 1923, a photo of himself with the words 'WANTED $2000 REWARD' printed in bold type around it.) Instead, Warhol created a vast mural comprising 22 canvases reproducing mug-shot photographs of 13 alleged criminals taken from the FBI's 'Most Wanted Men' posters openly displayed in US post offices; the work was entitled *Thirteen Most Wanted Men*. (The canvases reproduced here were offshoots of the World's Fair mural.)

Unfortunately for Warhol, however, only a few of the men represented in the mural were still wanted by the police, and predominantly they were of American-Italian extraction, so both of these factors led to complaints. Under pressure from Nelson Rockefeller, the New York State Governor, the director of the World's Fair, City Commissioner Robert Moses, ordered the removal of the mural. Warhol then proposed that he replace the images with pictures of Commissioner Moses himself, and even went ahead and made the Robert Moses paintings in his studio, but they never saw the light of day, for Philip Johnson refused to countenance such a substitution. As a result, Warhol simply obliterated the mural by having it painted over with aluminium paint. That effacement ties in with the artist's usual attitude towards negation, and it was an act that was certainly worthy of the Dadaists at their height, although indirectly Warhol had the last laugh, for ironically crime levels at the 1964 New York World's Fair broke all records.

Who are these men and what have they done or what are they accused of? Because we are not told of their supposed or real offences, they intrigue us all the more, for we can only attempt to guess their alleged or actual crimes from their physiognomies; such possible intrigue raises disturbing questions about our own motives for being drawn to this imagery, and once again Warhol has thereby brilliantly confronted us with basic problems of artistic rationale. The notion of using criminals or suspects as subjects for art wittily ties in with the subversive tactics of Dadaism, which again points to Warhol's strong affinity with that anti-artistic movement, and naturally, by employing criminal imagery in the first place, he was also taking his art into yet another major area of human experience.

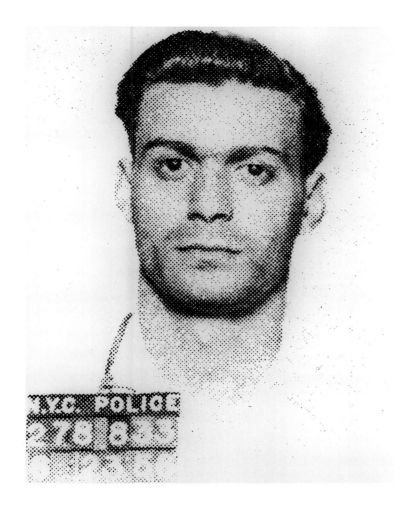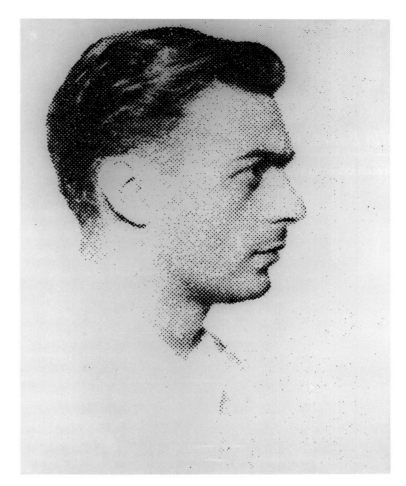
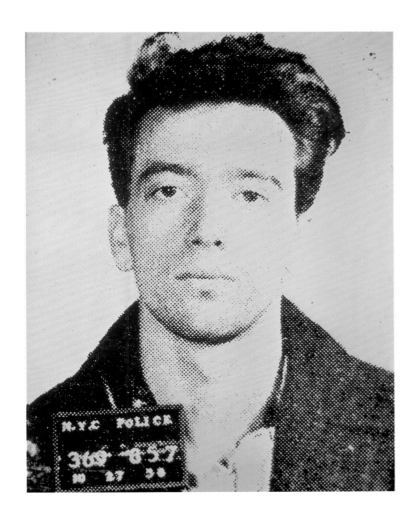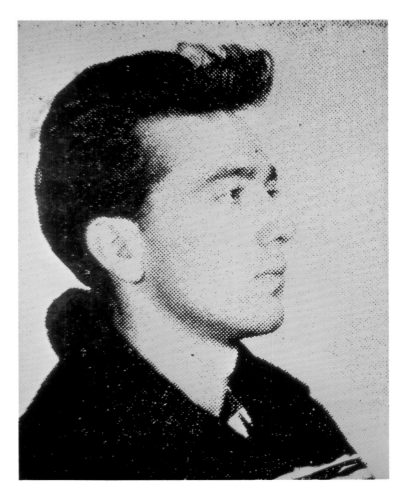

Brillo Boxes, 1964

Silkscreen ink on synthetic polymer paint on wood, each box 51 cm high × 51 cm wide × 43 cm deep. The Estate of Andy Warhol

This is a photograph of part of Warhol's packing carton sculptures exhibition held at the Stable Gallery, New York, in April 1964 (for another picture of the show see page 26). Warhol probably derived the idea for the display from the exhibitions of sculptures of everyday consumer goods held under the title of *Store* by Claes Oldenburg in 1961; Warhol is known to have visited one of the *Store* shows and been taken aback by it. Here, however, he gave us a somewhat more subversive and relentless project than Oldenburg's witty celebrations of consumerism.

For these works the designs of the cardboard outer packing cartons of Campbell's Tomato Juices, Del Monte Peach Halves, Mott's Apple Juices, Brillo Soap Pads, Heinz Ketchups and Kellogg's Cornflakes were silkscreened by Warhol and Gerard Malanga on all six sides of over 400 wooden boxes that had been made to order by a team of carpenters. It was certainly as valid for Warhol to imitate cheap packing cartons as it was, say, for ancient Greek sculptors to replicate the human body, and the boxes took to a logical conclusion the cultural implications of a painted bronze replica of two Ballantine beer cans that Jasper Johns had made in 1960, for by being created and displayed *en masse*, they raise even more pointed questions about the nature of appearance and reality, and about the commercial value of a work of art *versus* the object it represents. By almost filling the Stable Gallery with these sculptures Warhol was thereby converting the space into a glorified supermarket stockroom, and thus reminding us that art galleries are usually only glorified supermarket stockrooms anyway. Although Warhol had visions of purchasers carting away large numbers of the sculptures, sales were poor – for why spend money on these objects when you could get the real thing for nothing behind a supermarket? – and as a result Elinor Ward withdrew her backing from the painter, who moved to the Leo Castelli Gallery as a consequence.

The carton sculptures caused further cultural ructions early in 1965 when a Toronto art dealer attempted to import 80 of them for a show but was prevented from doing so by Canadian Customs officials who attempted to levy a hefty import duty on the objects as 'merchandise'; when the dealer appealed to the Director of the National Gallery of Canada to mediate on his behalf he was told that such artefacts were certainly not works of art. (Here North American art history repeated itself, but in reverse, for in 1926 the sculptor Constantin Brancusi had almost suffered the same fate at the hands of United States Customs officials with one of his *Bird in space* sculptures, although fortunately the matter was eventually resolved in his favour.)

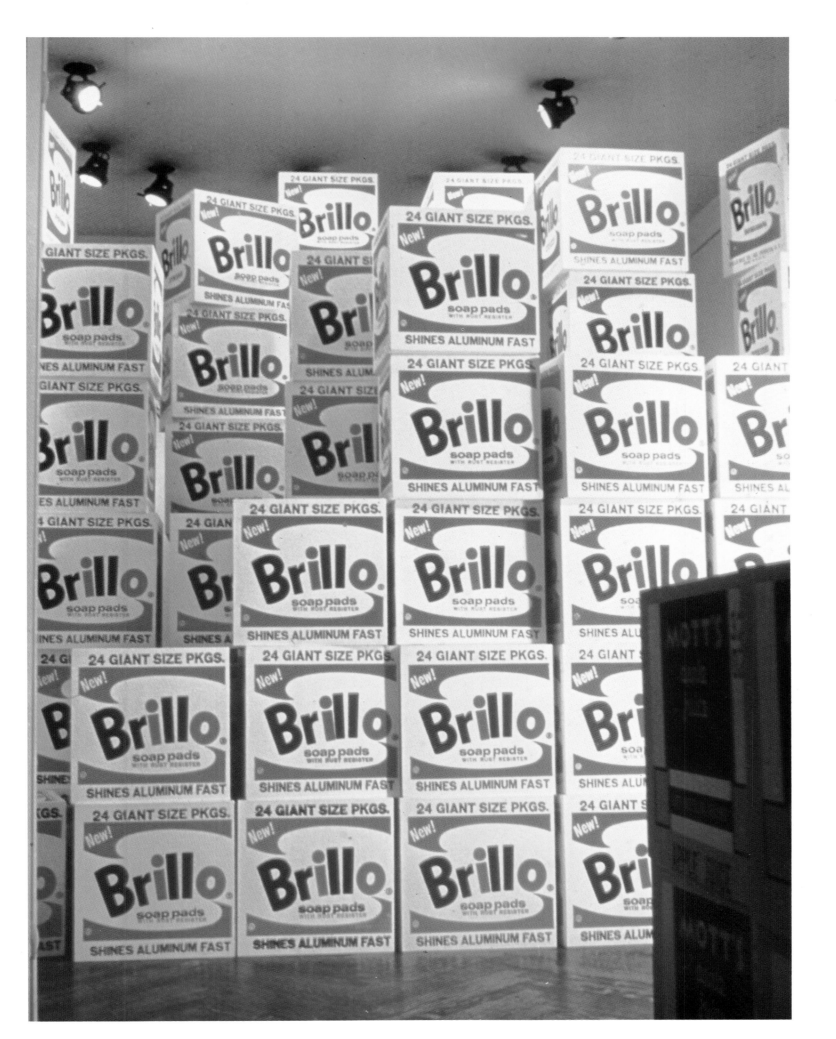

Flowers, 1964

Silkscreen ink on synthetic polymer paint on canvas, 293.4 × 293.4 cm. The Estate of Andy Warhol

In his *Flowers* paintings Warhol covered yet another major area of life and art, for flowers form a principal component of the natural world and there is a long and hallowed tradition of depicting blooms in Western painting. This series came about after Henry Geldzahler met Warhol in April 1964 at the New York World's Fair and suggested that, instead of producing any more Death and Disaster pictures, he should paint flowers instead. Warhol thereupon had sets of silkscreens made up from a photograph of some hibiscus flowers that he cropped and rearranged from the June 1964 edition of *Modern Photography* magazine. Assisted by Gerard Malanga, he made over 900 flower paintings that summer (although he forgot to obtain permission to reproduce the original flower photograph before doing so and was successfully sued for breach of copyright by the photographer, Patricia Caulfield). The vast replication of the images surely makes the point that in the present era the natural world has become prettified, commodified and marketed on a mass scale, a prettification, commodification and marketing that were paralleled by Warhol himself, for the first exhibition of the Flowers paintings at the Leo Castelli Gallery in November 1964 was a sell-out.

The original photograph in *Modern Photography* adorned an article on variations in colour printing, and so Warhol's great number of colour variations in his Flowers paintings is very apt. Because of the formal repetitiveness and colour variation, the works almost function simultaneously as investigations into the ways that such stresses and changes alter our perceptions of form, which could conceivably have been one of Warhol's ancillary intentions, given his highly developed visual sensibility. And as usual, the painter's alertness to the intrinsic visual properties of forms made him push the shapes of the flowers to the interface with abstraction, although the bland, flattened colour areas of the petals themselves equally suggest that the flowers have been processed, as though they were somehow mass-produced (which in reality, of course, they are, although by natural forces). Moreover, the sense of abstraction in these forms is certainly heightened by the repetitiousness, crowding and colour variation of the flowers if they are seen *en masse*, as they were in the Castelli Gallery show, and again at the Ileana Sonnabend Gallery in Paris in May 1965. Warhol chose to display such pictures in Paris at the time because, as he commented in *POPism: The Warhol '60s*:

> In France they weren't interested in new art; they'd gone back to liking the Impressionists mostly. That's what made me decide to send them the Flowers; I figured they'd like that.

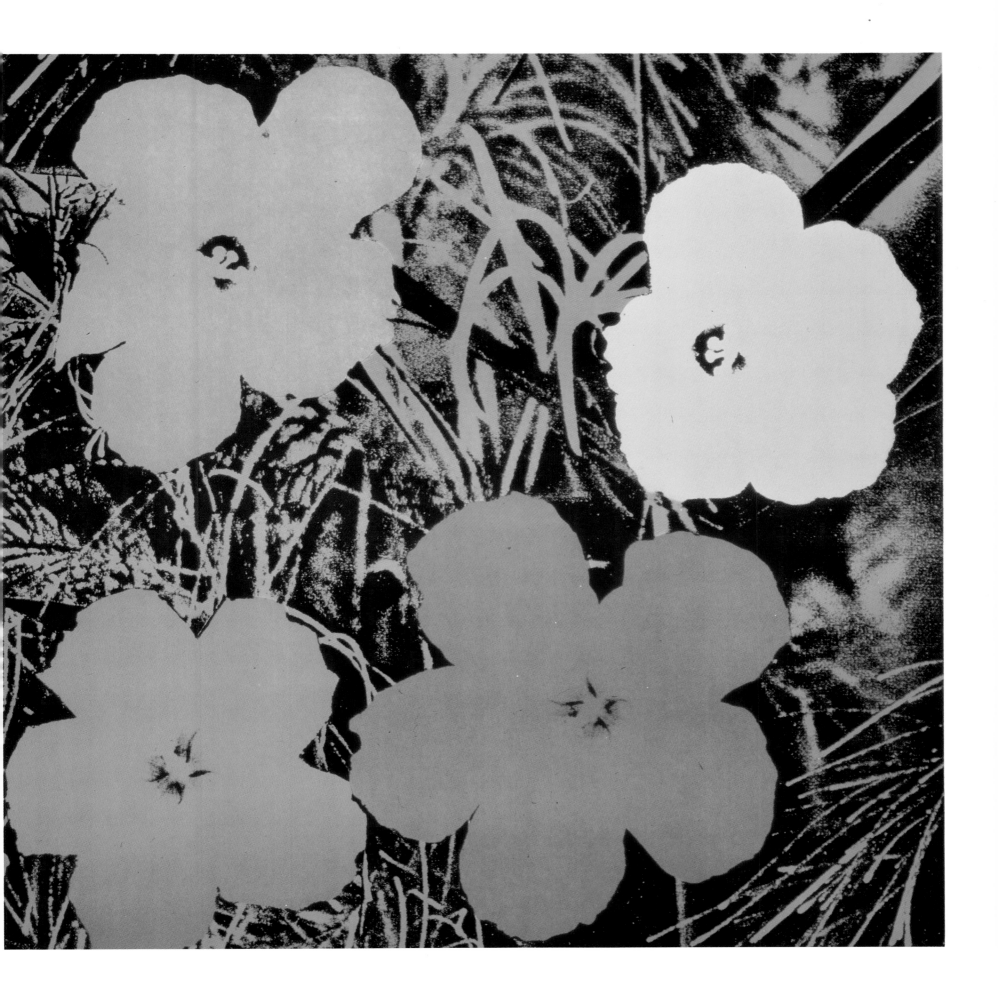

Jackie, 1964

Silkscreen ink on synthetic polymer paint on 35 canvases, 40.6 × 50.8 cm each. Museum of Modern Art, Frankfurt-am-Main

Rhythm is the keynote of this most formally cohesive of all the portraits of Jacqueline Kennedy that Warhol embarked upon shortly after the assassination of John F. Kennedy in November 1963. The original photograph that provided the image was taken aboard the presidential aircraft on the evening after the shooting, when Kennedy's shocked widow stood beside Lyndon B. Johnson and his wife as the Vice-President was sworn in as President on the flight back to Washington. Warhol refused to grieve overly for the dead president, however, for as he commented in *POPism: The Warhol '60s*:

> I'd been thrilled having Kennedy as president; he was handsome, young, smart – but it didn't bother me that much that he was dead. What bothered me was the way the television and radio were programming everybody to feel so sad.

Such programming is indirectly suggested by the use of a repetitiousness that simultaneously reminds us of the way that the mass-communications media originally sent Jackie Kennedy's pained likeness through a multitude of electric and printed conduits to the world. And once again Warhol's propensity to enjoy the best of two worlds is evident, for through the use of visual rhythm the imagery approaches the condition of abstraction.

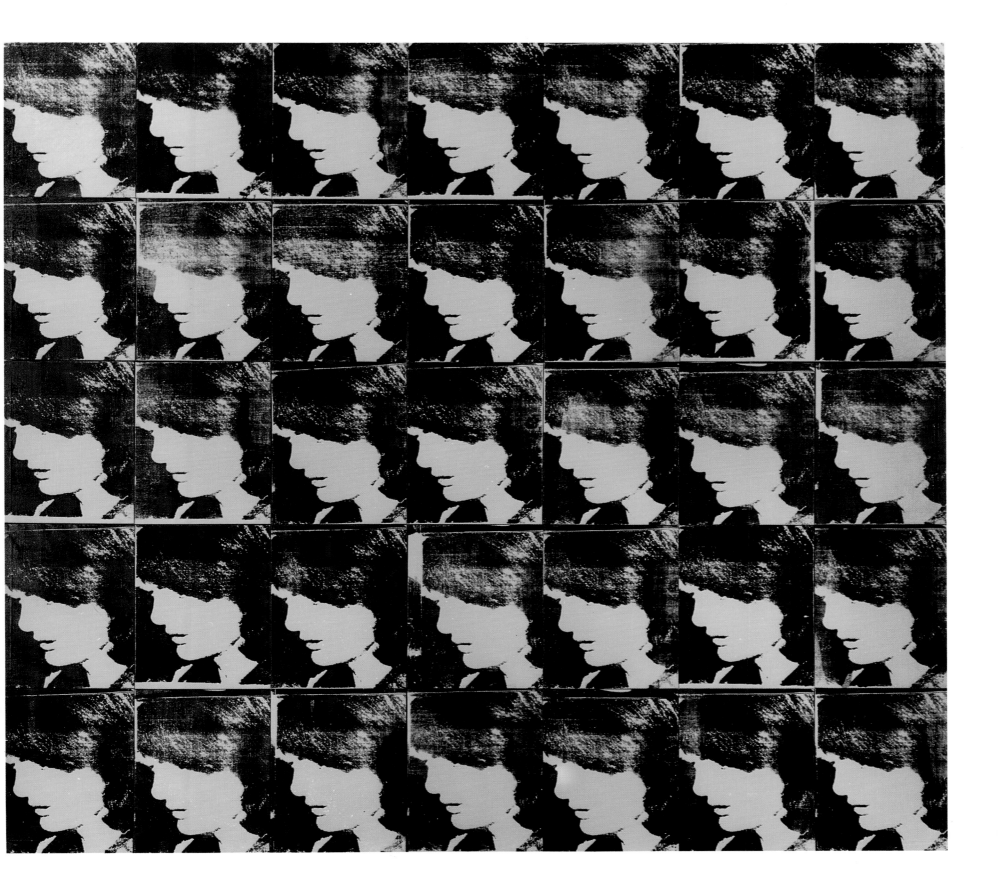

Campbell's Soup Multicoloured, 1965

Silkscreen ink on synthetic polymer paint on canvas, 91.7 × 60.9 cm. Museum of Modern Art, New York (Philip Johnson Fund)

This is another of Warhol's statements about departure from a norm, for when the painter made a new sequence of Campbell's soup-can paintings in 1965, they were coloured in hues that would never have been encountered on real Campbell's soup-cans in a supermarket. The colour relationships in these paintings demonstrate yet again that Warhol was a born colourist (if not even a sensualist) beneath his artificial, emotionally neutral veneer, while ultimately these works make the age-old point that an artist does not have to accept reality just as he or she finds it; they are free to transcend the limitations of 'normal' appearances.

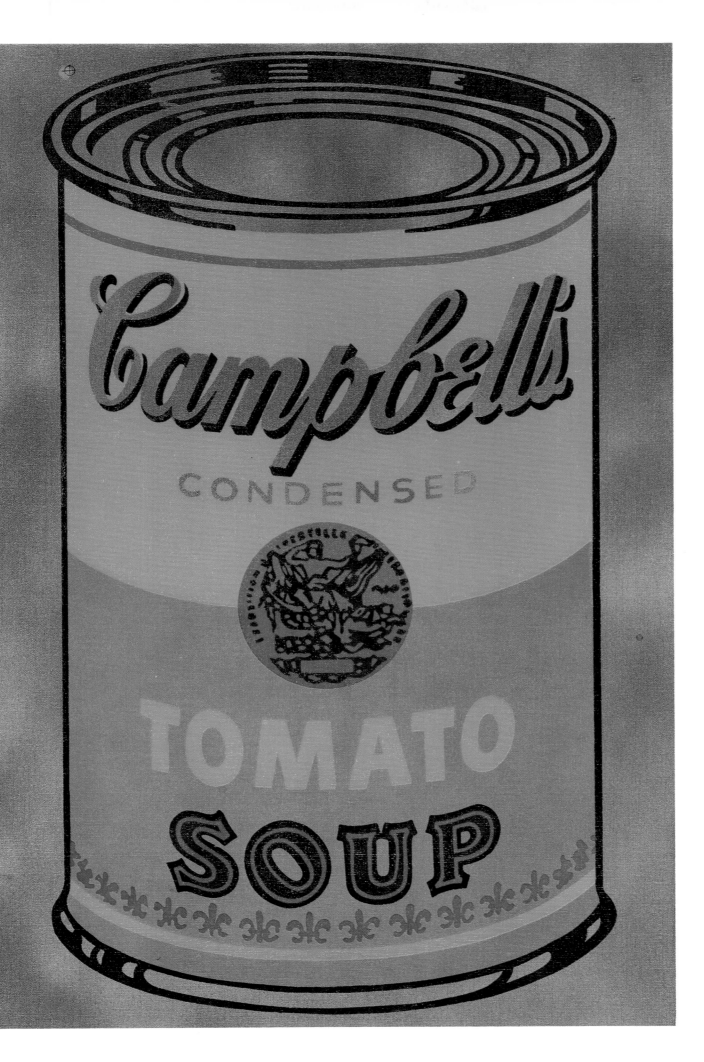

Cow Wallpaper, 1966

Silkscreen on wallpaper, 115.5 × 75.5 cm. The Estate of Andy Warhol

Here we see just one section of a printed design that originally was repeated vertically in strips as a wallpaper. That wallpaper developed logically from the wallpaper-effect that the Flowers paintings had made when shown *en masse* in New York in 1964 and in Paris in 1965, and it was used to cover the walls of one of two rooms in the Leo Castelli Gallery Warhol exhibition in April 1966. Unfortunately only a few of the rolls of wallpaper were sold, thus bringing about a rupture between the artist and Leo Castelli (and also now making the few surviving rolls very rare indeed). But the wallpaper could never have functioned as a proper wallpaper anyway, for as Charles F. Stuckey has pointed out, 'Its left side does not interlock graphically with its right side as repeat patterns must. Instead, Warhol's *Cow Wallpaper* is like a printed film strip of a close-up shot for one of his motionless movies'.

As narrated in the Introduction (p. 30), Warhol derived the notion of making images of cows from Ivan Karp, who felt that nobody dealt with pastoral imagery any more. And like the Flowers paintings, the *Cow Wallpaper* operates on a variety of levels: it links with – and perhaps sums up – the pastoral tradition in Western art; it points up the repetitiousness through which generally we now experience nature 'in the comfort of our own homes'; it makes the point that in the modern world, painting has usually become just so much cultural wallpaper, and sometimes pretty dumb wallpaper at that; and it connects very strongly with the Dada tradition of subverting our notion of what constitutes a work of art, let alone the validity of art itself.

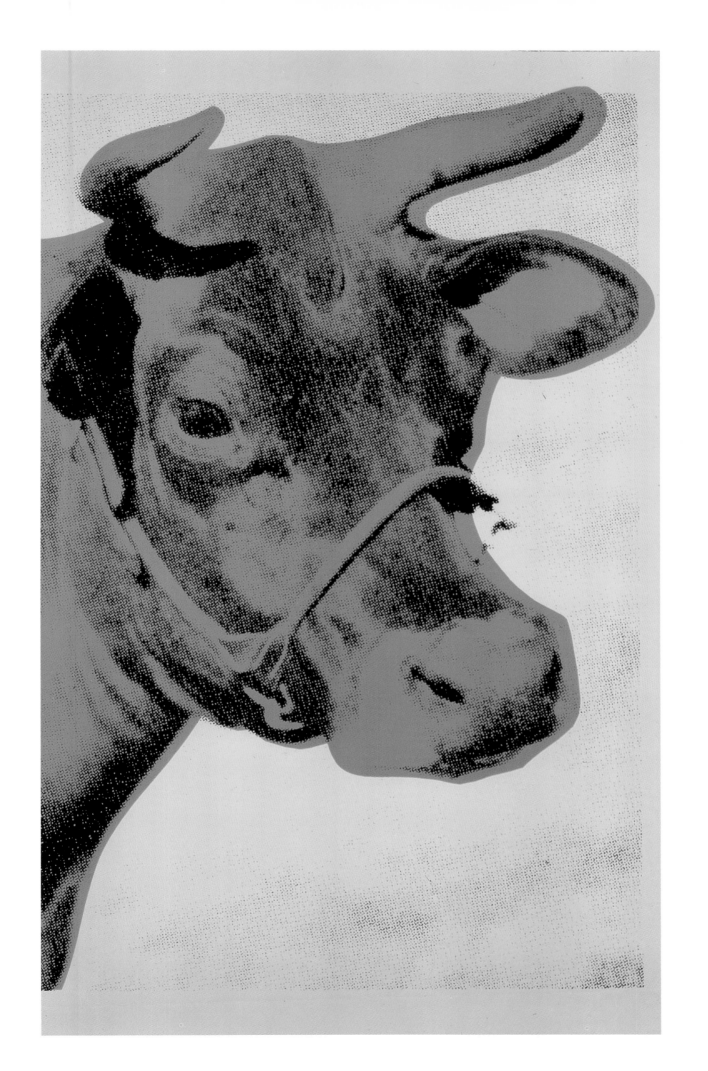

Marilyn, 1967

Screenprints on paper, each 91.5 × 91.5 cm. The Estate of Andy Warhol

Although Warhol had made a number of individual screenprints on paper before 1967, it was logical for him eventually to exploit the medium more fully by creating series of prints devoted to a single theme, and thus open up a much wider and more financially accessible market than the one enjoyed by his paintings. And given the popularity of the Marilyn pictures, those images were an obvious choice for the painter's first series of prints. There are ten prints in this suite, although for reasons of space only nine are reproduced here.

Once again Warhol's characteristic tendency to stress the innate abstraction of things is apparent in these works, for the prints function efficiently as a series of investigations into the nature of colour relationships, whilst doubling as comments upon the occasional deformations of colour printing. And in addition to the breakdown into yellow hair, green eyelids, ruby lips and pink skin that is familiar from many of the Marilyn paintings, there are also a number of unusual colour arrangements that impart a wholly different and even unfamiliar slant to the image, if not even deform or mask it, as with the green, pink and red polarized version which renders the face difficult to see. Such perceptual difficulties prefigure the camouflaging that Warhol would explore near the end of his life.

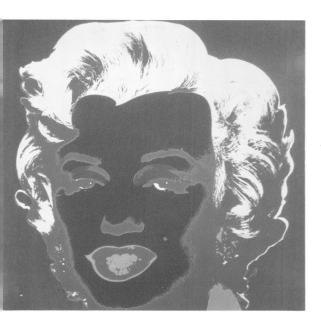 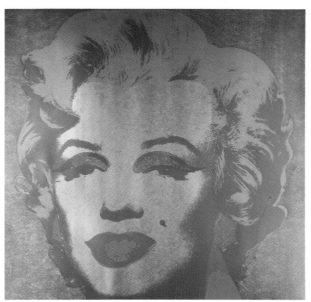 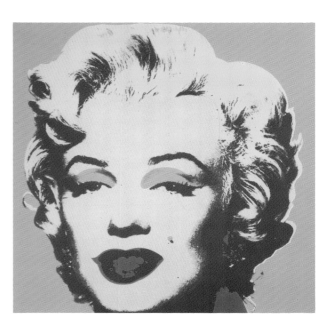

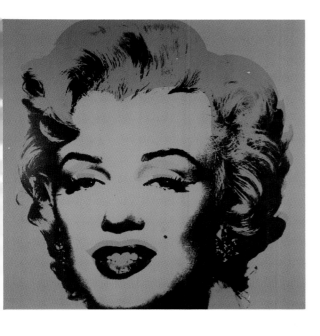 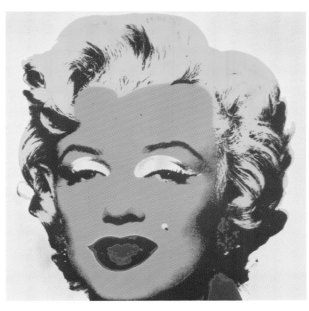 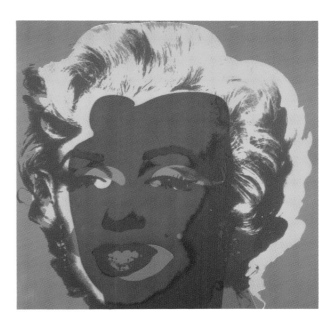

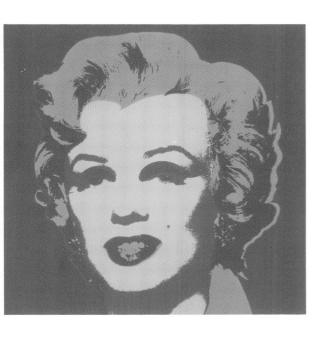 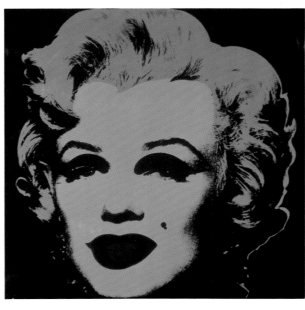 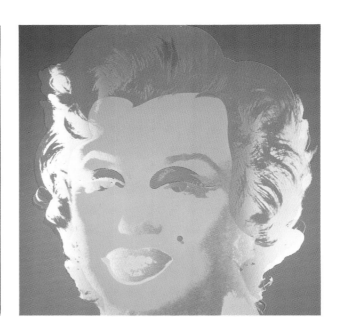

Chairman Mao, 1974

This colour photograph shows the exhibition of the *Chairman Mao* paintings at the Musée Galleria in Paris in February–March 1974.

Warhol took his image of the politician from the frontispiece portrait in the little red book, *The Thoughts of Chairman Mao*, and that appropriation was a brilliant stroke of irony on his part, for although 1971–2 saw a major thaw in relations between the United States and China, nonetheless the Chinese leader still represented everything that was antithetical to American capitalism. The notion that wealthy Americans and other financial fat cats might decorate their homes with the beaming visage of someone whose life had been dedicated to the eradication of everything they stood for must have struck Warhol as being rather funny, as indeed it is. And the irony was culturally doubled when Warhol produced a *Chairman Mao* wallpaper to act as a backdrop for the hanging of the *Chairman Mao* paintings in exhibitions, as here, for like the dumb-looking animal in *Cow Wallpaper*, the endless heads point up the contemporary background role of much art, while equally projecting a universe filled with unutterably blank-looking images. By this means, Warhol was clearly making larger points about political idolatry and the seemingly endless visual repetitiousness that it can often sadly lead to.

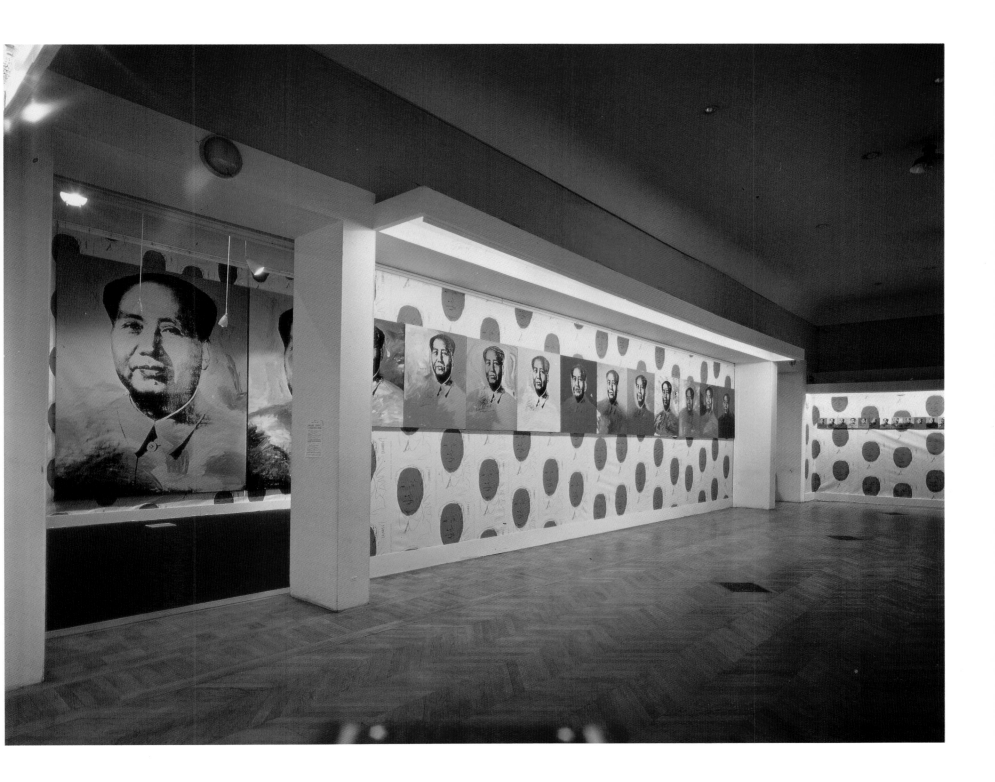

Chairman Mao, 1972

Silkscreen ink on synthetic polymer paint on canvas, 448.3 × 346 cm. Saatchi Collection, London

With the odd exception, like the *Red Race Riot* discussed above (p. 71), between about 1961 and 1966 Warhol went out of his way to obtain the maximum degree of surface flatness in his paintings; to that end the inherent flattening effect of silkscreen printing over painted underlays aided him enormously, although the pictures of that period do retain a certain surface vibrancy because of the grainy tooth of the canvas itself. Such flatness may be seen as Warhol's way of achieving the maximum degree of impersonality in his works, and equally as an alternative to the emotionalism that was often expressed through thickly worked paint-surfaces by the previous generation of New York school abstract painters. But by the end of the 1960s Warhol began to use paint more thickly and, like many of the portraits that he made after this date, the *Chairman Mao* pictures demonstrate an increased painterliness as the artist worked up a thick facture of paint across each canvas before overprinting the final photo-silkscreened portrait image. Probably this painterliness was Warhol's way of reinvesting the act of painting with some validity, for of course the major physical and sensory (not to mention sensual) difference between painting and photography resides in such a tactile emphasis, although as we shall see with the next picture to be discussed, gestural painterliness can look merely rhetorical unless it serves greater dramatic and expressive ends.

As already noted, in the *Chairman Mao* series Warhol engineered (and continues to bring about) a richly ironic appropriation of a communist holy icon by western capitalist art-lovers. In this particular painting the use of yellow for the underpainted flesh tones may have been intended subtly to augment that irony by inducing associations of the 'yellow menace' that Chinese communism had once additionally represented in some of the more populist American mass-communications media at an earlier moment in history, most notably during the Korean war period of the 1950s.

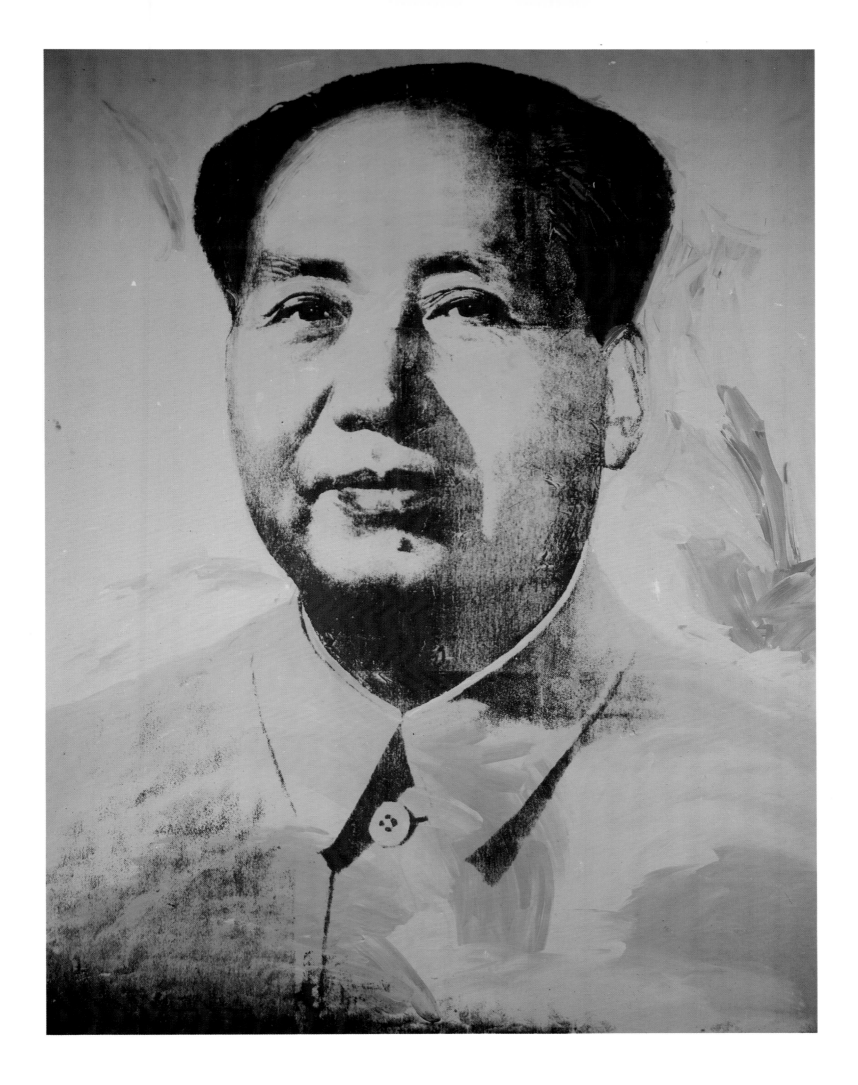

Julia Warhola, 1974

Synthetic polymer silkscreened on canvas, 101.5 × 101.5 cm. The Estate of Andy Warhol

It may be that Warhol had some commemorative purpose in painting a number of pictures of his mother shortly after her decease in 1972, but other than remembrance itself it is difficult to discern what that purpose could have been, for despite the apparent dynamism of their surfaces, the works lack dramatic point. This is because the dynamism has nothing much to do; the thick paint simply swirls around or under the images of Julia Warhola without deepening our insight into her personality or even the painter's reaction to her. When Warhol used portraiture to make telling cultural points, as he had done in the highly ironic *Chairman Mao* images, the failure to relate painterly means to dramatic ends does not really matter, for the implications of the imagery carry the flaccid underlying painterliness with them. But when any such larger dramatic purpose is apparently absent (as here), the painterliness merely appears turgid rather than expressive, if not even emptily rhetorical and messy; in pictures like these, Warhol had returned full circle to the unconvincing, affected painterliness evident in his art around 1960–1, when he had married popular imagery with a synthetic expressionism.

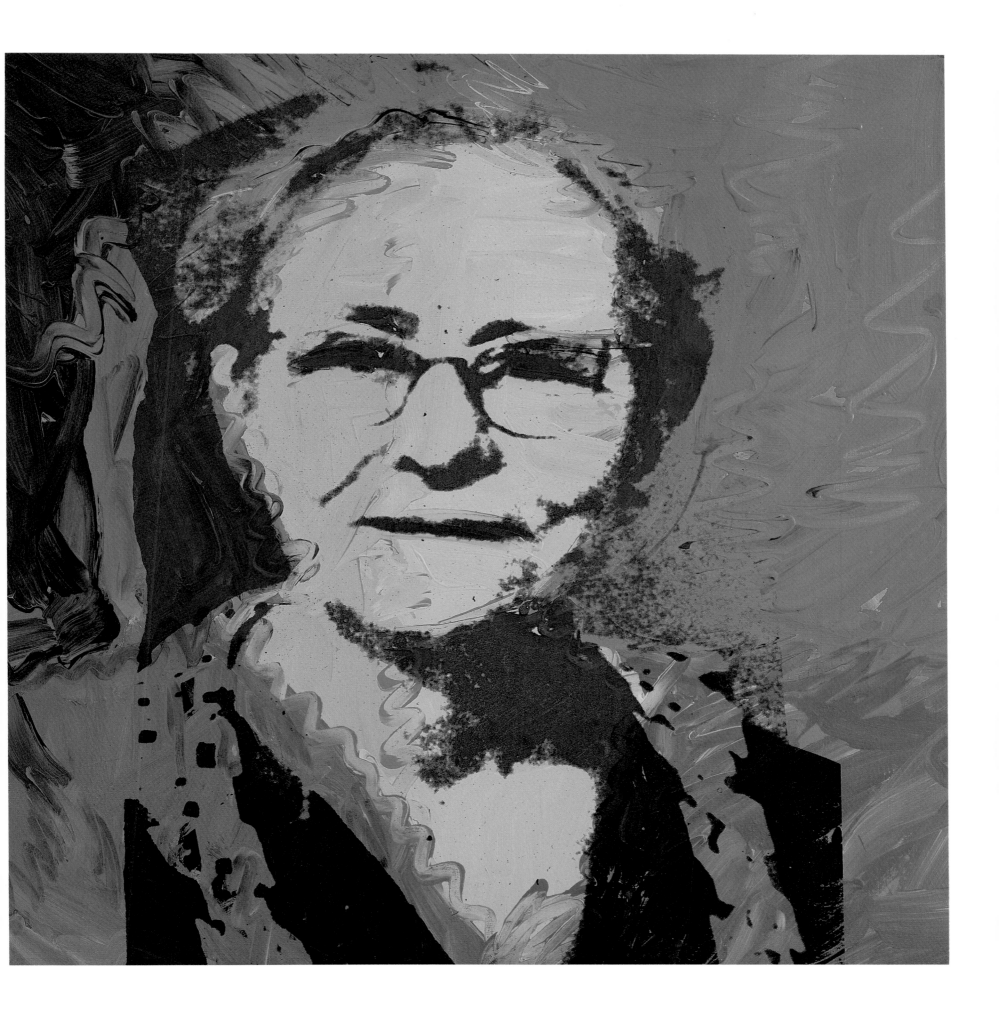

Skull, 1976

Silkscreen ink on synthetic polymer paint on canvas, 38.1 × 48.3 cm. The Estate of Andy Warhol

Despite Warhol's customary declaration that there were no meanings behind the surfaces of his works, the Skulls series of paintings again demonstrates his underlying seriousness of purpose. The images were made from photographs of a skull that the painter had bought in a Paris flea market around 1975, and he was encouraged to develop the series by Fred Hughes, who reminded him that artists like Zurbarán and Picasso had used such objects to great expressive effect. Moreover, Warhol's studio assistant, Ronnie Cutrone (who became his professional helper in 1974), also encouraged him to use the skull by remarking that it would be 'like doing the portrait of everybody in the world'.

At Warhol's behest, Cutrone took a great many monochrome photographs of the skull from a number of different angles, lighting it harshly and from the side so as to obtain the most dramatic visual effects through maximizing the shadows thrown by the object, and its light and dark contrasts. In most of the Skulls images (as here), the use of vivid colours tends to glamorize the object, and that glamorization is highly ironic, given the way that the leering skull points up the superficiality of glamour: in the midst of life we are in death indeed, as Andy Warhol the media Superstar was only too painfully aware after 1968.

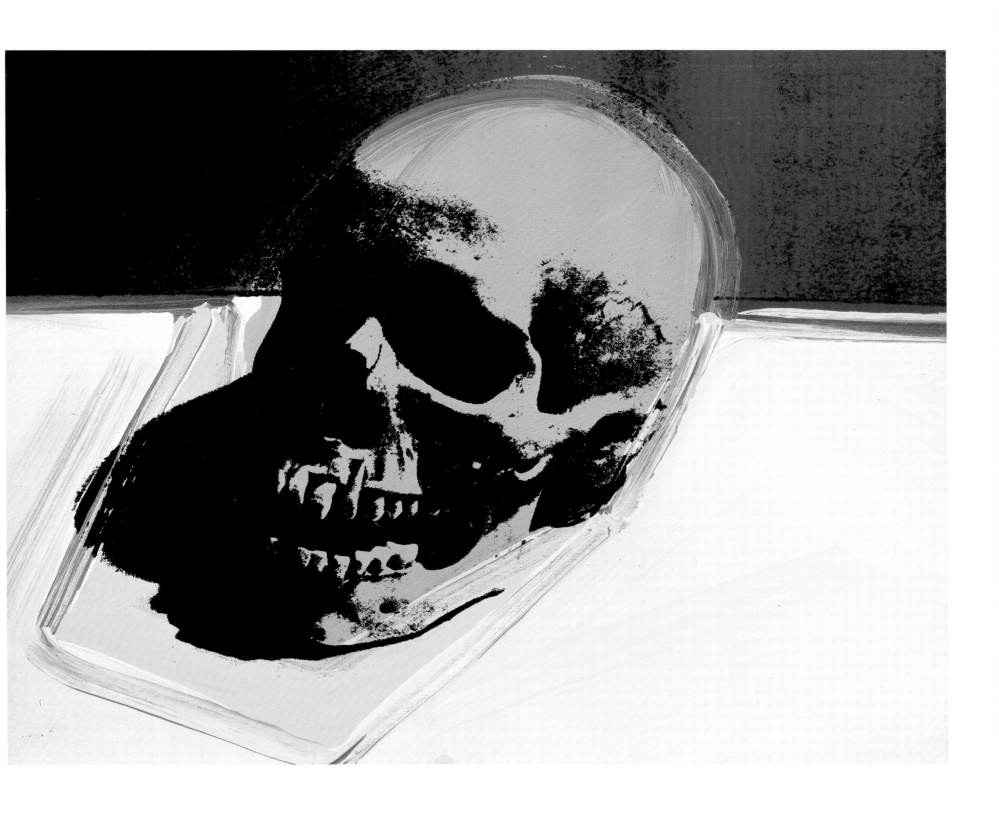

Hammer and Sickle, 1977

Watercolour on paper, 71.1 × 102.9 cm. The Estate of Andy Warhol

More irony in the vein of the Chairman Mao images, as Warhol presented the capitalist art market with communist symbols for its delectation. These images had their origins in a 1976 visit to Italy, where the painter frequently saw the symbols of industrial and agrarian power scribbled on walls; as he later told Ronnie Cutrone:

> Gee, when you walk around Italy, all over the walls no matter where you go, there in chalk or paint, there's all these images scribbled on everything with hammers and sickles . . .

Back in New York, Warhol had Cutrone fruitlessly scour left-wing stores in search of three-dimensional hammer and sickle symbols for subsequent use in pictures; in the end Cutrone simply bought brand-new hammers and sickles from a hardware store, and then photographed them many times.

This is one of several watercolours that Warhol made whilst he was producing a series of silkscreen paintings of the same subject, although in both drawings and paintings he played freely with the forms of the hammers and sickles in a characteristic exploration of the intrinsic abstract qualities of the shapes of such objects. All his old graphic skilfulness can be seen in the present work, where clearly he relished the contrast between the objects and the shadows they throw, a pointer to the Shadows series of wholly abstract images that was soon to follow.

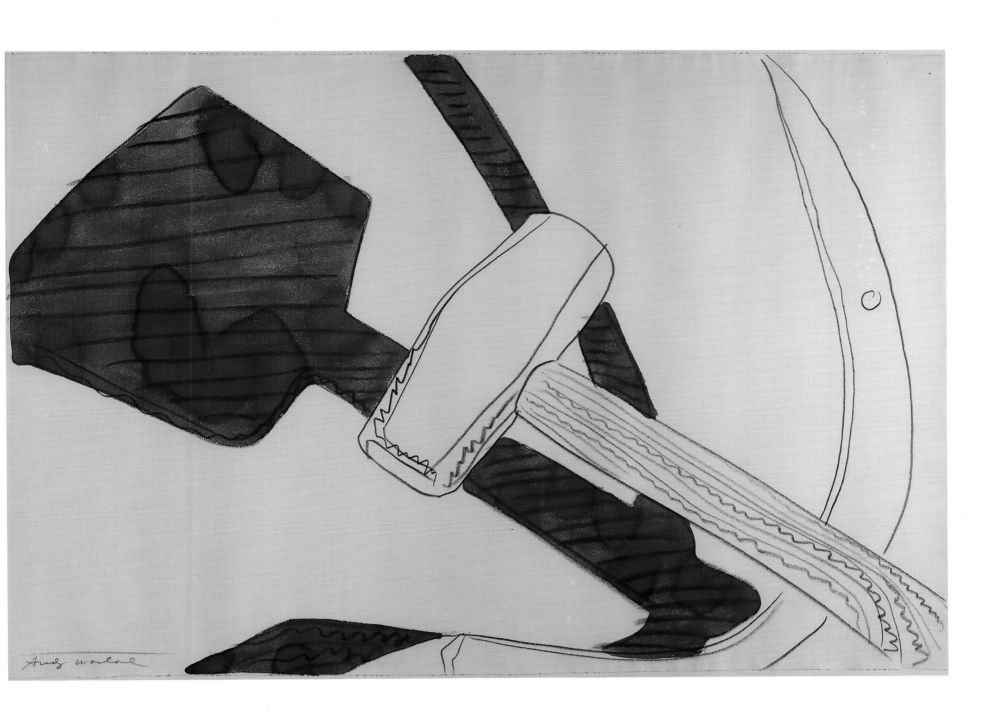

Shadows, 1978

Silkscreen ink on synthetic polymer paint on canvas, 102 canvases, each 193 × 132.1 cm. Dia Art Foundation, New York

This photograph shows the installation of the Shadows paintings at 393 West Broadway, New York, in January 1979. The pictures were made using photographs that Ronnie Cutrone had taken of fragments of cardboard; like the Skulls, these were dramatically lit so as to cast long shadows and enjoy a sharp division between light and shade.

Warhol claimed that these paintings were simply 'disco decor', as disco music was played at the party held for the opening of the 1979 New York exhibition. However, there are a number of reasons to take the works a little more seriously than that. As we have already seen, Warhol always felt an affinity with abstract painting, even if that attraction usually found expression through pushing representational imagery to the interface with abstraction rather than going beyond it. But rather than working purely as abstract paintings – and not very good ones at that, for there is little if any correspondence here between form and emotional expression, which is surely the point of gestural abstract painting like this – the very abstraction itself is presumably its own point, especially in the artistic context and on the scale in which the paintings were first shown, for they may represent the painter's comment on the limitations of abstract art.

One of the ways that many non-representational painters project a sense of visual identity is through creating series of repetitious forms, and here Warhol may have been simply taking to its logical conclusion that tendency of abstract works to look uniform. It is also possible that he was paying homage to Robert Rauschenberg when doing so, for he may well have seen the latter artist's *White Paintings* (dating from around 1949) when they toured various American museums between 1976 and 1978; these works are simply blank images designed to allow shadows to play across them, and in his paintings Warhol was instead fixing those transient shapes. And ultimately the fact that Warhol called these works 'Shadows' rather than, say, 'abstract paintings', perhaps makes a dramatic point, for shadows are by their very nature fleeting and have long been employed metaphorically in both painting and literature to denote the transience of life; through their use Warhol was surely projecting such an awareness also. That reading is certainly encouraged by the many nihilistic and death-filled statements that may be found elsewhere in Warhol's oeuvre.

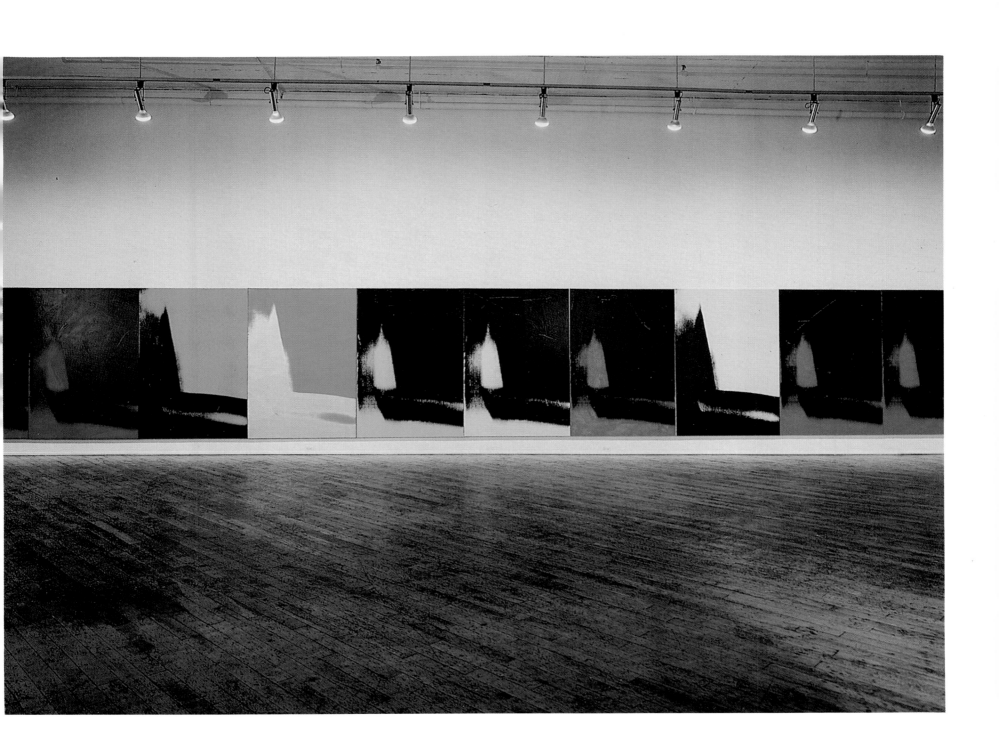

Truman Capote, 1979

Silkscreen ink on synthetic polymer paint on canvas, oo × oo cm. The Estate of Andy Warhol

On his very first visit to New York in 1948 Warhol formed a crush on Truman Capote after seeing the author's photograph on the back of his first book, *Other Voices, Other Rooms*. When the artist settled in New York soon afterwards he pestered his way into acquaintanceship with the writer, although Capote never regarded him highly in return and did little to encourage the relationship. However, Warhol persisted in his adulation and it was with a group of '15 Drawings Based on the Writings of Truman Capote' that he held his first exhibition in June 1952, a show that Capote eventually visited. In 1956 Warhol also made a shoe 'portrait' of Capote which he exhibited in his Crazy Golden Slippers show at the Bodley Gallery. Later, when he had achieved worldwide fame, he enjoyed a more equal relationship with the writer, eventually even employing him on *Interview* magazine when Capote's career was on the wane due to his failing literary powers and related alcoholism.

In other contemporaneous portraits of Capote using the same photo-silkscreened image, Warhol tonally emphasized the flat areas of supporting colour so as to make the staring eyes the focal point of the design and thereby increase their haunted, fixed look. Here, however, the flesh areas of cool blue set off by contrast the strident key of the yellow hat which serves to make a somewhat more fashion-conscious and glamorous statement about the author.

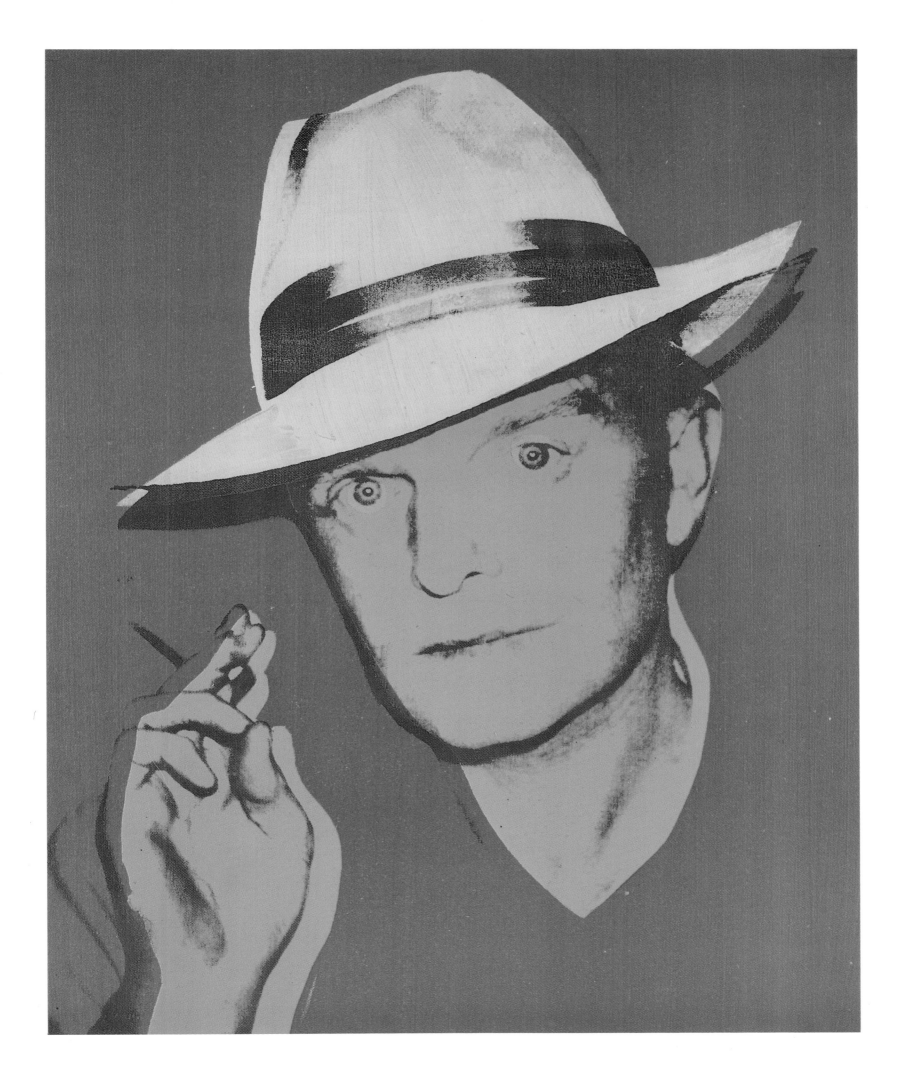

Eighteen Multi-Coloured Marilyns (Reversals Series), 1979–86

Silkscreen ink on synthetic polymer paint on canvas, 137 × 208 cm. Galerie Bruno Bischofberger, Zurich

In the Reversals series the painter recycled images he had earlier used but in a negative way akin to a photographic negative and often with a supporting underlay of colour, as here. It has been plausibly suggested by Nan Rosenthal that in doing so Warhol was drawing upon memories of juxtaposed positive and negative photographs that he remembered from Laszlo Moholy-Nagy's book *Vision in Motion*, which he is known to have read when he was an art student in Pittsburgh in the 1940s. In the Introduction (p. 38), it is suggested that conceptually the Reversals pictures are dramatically of a piece with the Shadows paintings that preceded them and with the contemporaneous Retrospectives series paintings, because of the fact that in all three series the painter subtly expressed facets of a related outlook: in the Shadows he underlined the fleeting nature of things; in the Reversals we are made aware of the dark side of things; and in the Retrospectives Warhol addressed the passing of things.

In the Reversals series the visual negativism directly parallels the emotional and spiritual negativism that Warhol apprehended in the world around him. And yet, paradoxically, this visual negativism is not without its positive dimension, for these images certainly enjoy a dynamic pictorial vivacity, although that vivacity might seem nightmarish, if not even hallucinatory. Moreover, the negativism and abiding darkness spark off a number of pertinent associations. For example, Marilyn Monroe was primarily known to the world through photographs that derive from negatives, while the large-scale replication of imagery such as we see here also parallels the way that photographs of Marilyn are endlessly multiplied in reality. And then there is the contrast between the brilliant colours and the surrounding blackness. We have already noted Warhol's ironic conjunction of glamorous colours with a superimposed image of death in the Skulls paintings, and here too exactly the same moral conjunction of glamour and darkness may have been intended, but with death represented by the dead Marilyn instead.

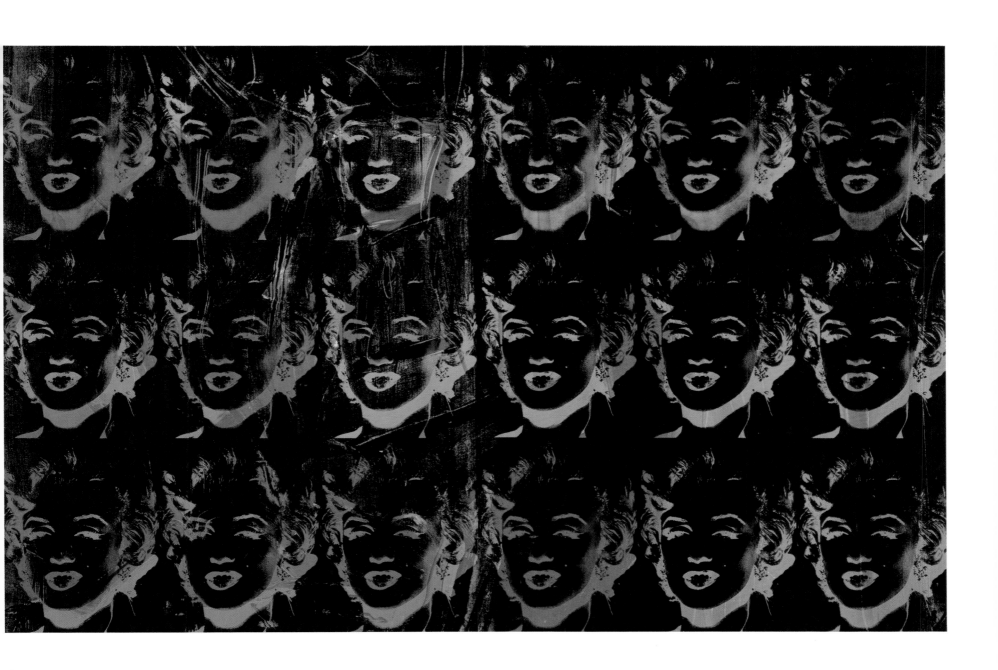

Diamond Dust Joseph Beuys, 1980

Silkscreen ink and synthetic diamond dust on synthetic polymer paint on canvas, 254 × 203.2 cm. Marx Collection, Berlin

Joseph Beuys (1921–86) was perhaps the most influential of post-war German sculptors and conceptual artists, and by the time of his death he was also financially the most highly valued artist in the world, something that certainly appealed to Warhol (who was not far behind him in the league table of artistic top earners). Beuys was also one of the founders of the German Green movement, and he was especially brilliant at communicating through the mass media. He first met Warhol in New York in 1979, and the American artist was commissioned to paint his portrait the following year; later he went on to create further images of Beuys, including sets of silkscreen prints, published between 1980 and 1983, as well as a portrait entitled *Joseph Beuys in Memoriam* created after the sculptor's death, in which a positive rendition of the head is overlaid with camouflaged patternings. Warhol had a low opinion of Beuys's work, but the German sculptor esteemed Warhol highly for the conceptual complexity of his art, and the two exhibited their works alongside each other in Berlin in 1982 when the Marx collection – to which this portrait belongs – went on display in the National Gallery there.

This is yet another of Warhol's reversals images, and the marriage of negativism and glamour that we have noted elsewhere in the Skulls and Reversals series pictures was effected here not through combining a negative portrait image with an underpainting of garish colours but instead by the sprinkling of synthetic diamond dust over the image whilst the silkscreen ink was still wet, thus bonding the two together. Although it is unfortunately difficult to see in reproduction, in reality the diamond dust gives off a brilliant glitter that introduces potent associations of a showbiz glitziness entirely and wittily appropriate to Beuys's role as an art-world superstar.

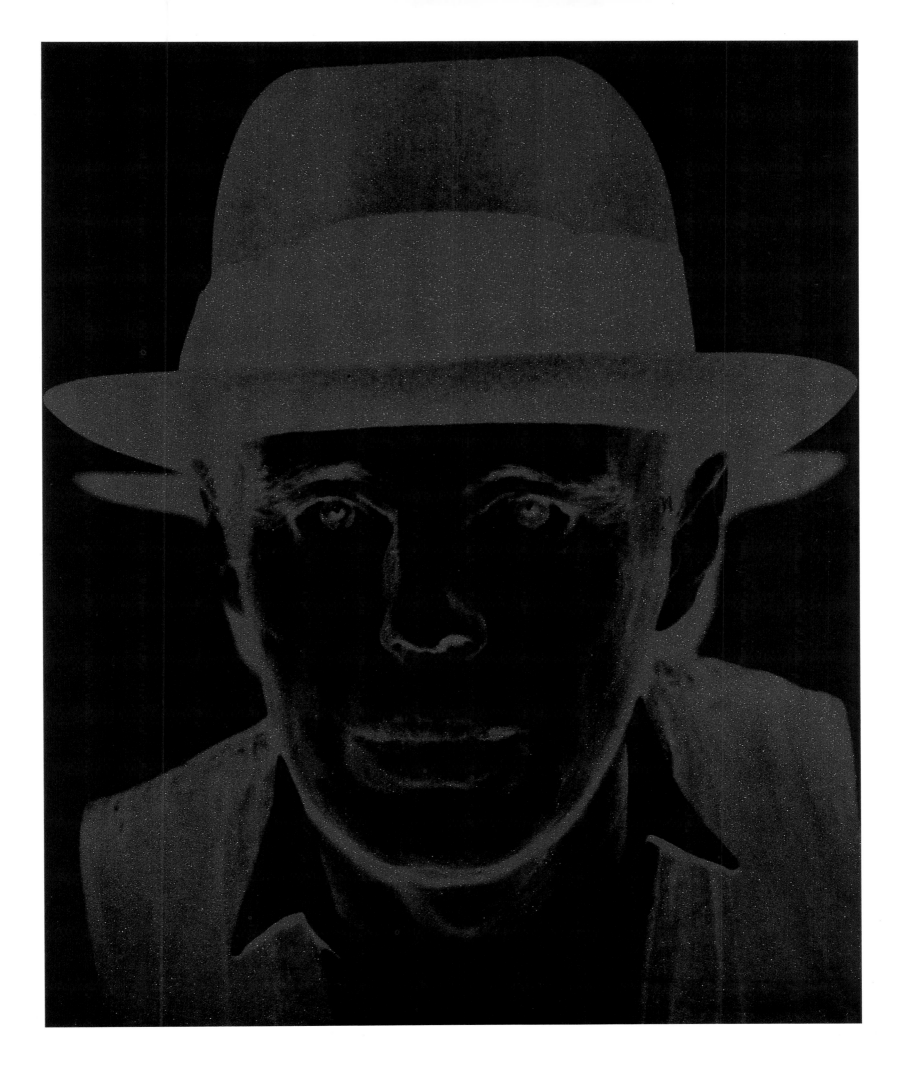

Dollar Signs, 1981

Synthetic polymer paint and silkscreen ink on canvas, 228.6 × 177.8 cm. Leo Castelli Gallery, New York

In his book, *The Philosophy of Andy Warhol*, the painter stated:

> I like money on the wall. Say you were going to buy a $200,000 painting. I think you should take that money, tie it up, and hang it on the wall. Then when someone visited you the first thing they would see is the money on the wall.

Here Warhol gives us both the painting and the money on the wall. Yet although the symbols of value may have changed, in this image made from drawings that Warhol had produced himself, the artist covered identical conceptual ground to that of the Dollar Bills series of pictures of the early 1960s, with the same ironic unmasking of art-as-money, for what better and more congruent denotations of the objects of their desires could art-capitalists want to hang on their walls than pictures like these, works, moreover, that would hopefully be increasing in value all the time?

Yet despite such irony, perhaps it was the fact that Warhol was going over old ground that led to the commercial failure of the Dollar Signs pictures when they were first exhibited at one of Leo Castelli's downtown galleries in New York in January 1982, for critical responses were very negative and none of them sold. In the original hanging of the show, Ronnie Cutrone had judiciously mixed the Dollar Signs with contemporaneous pictures of Guns and Knives, but the hanging did not appeal to Fred Hughes who replaced the weaponry images with just the money-symbol pictures. (A later show of all three types of images mixed with representations of religious crosses, held in Madrid at the end of 1982, was a sell-out, however.) The financial failure of the Dollar Signs show led to further difficulties in Warhol's relationship with Leo Castelli.

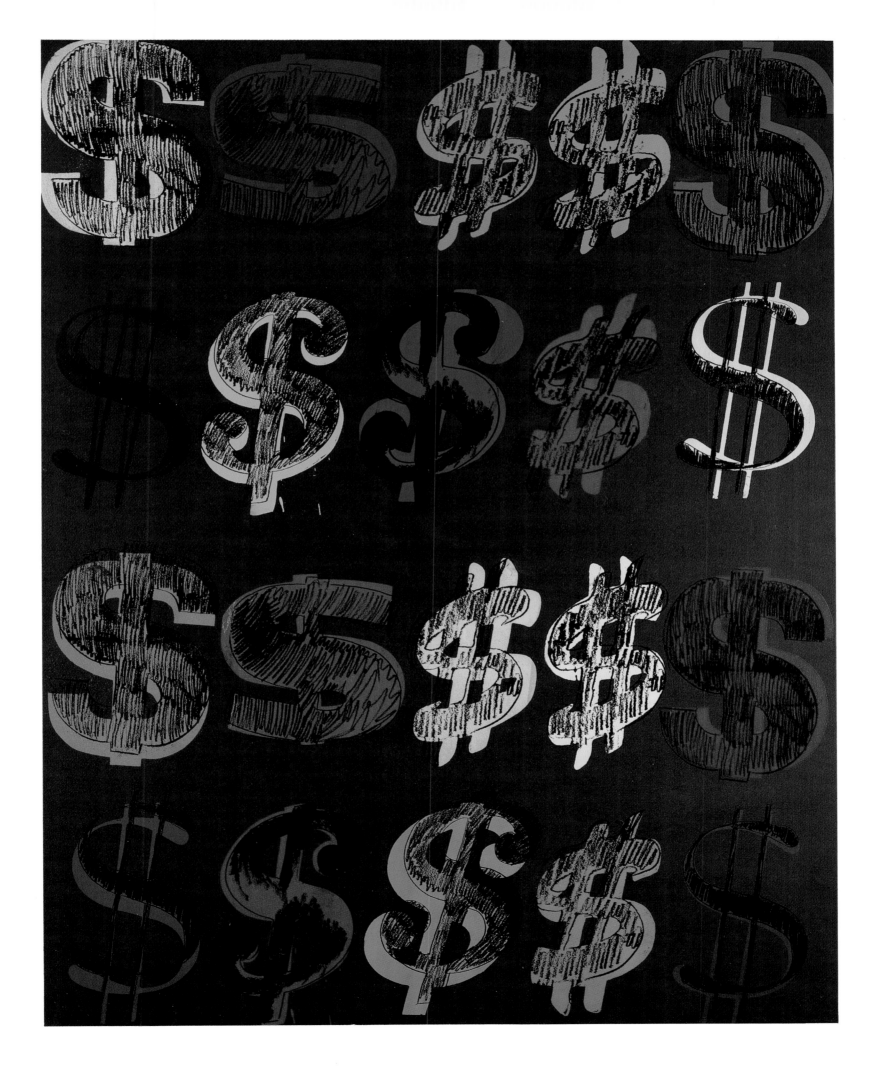

Guns, 1981

Silkscreen ink on synthetic polymer paint on canvas, 40.6 × 50.8 cm. The Estate of Andy Warhol

Given the personal suffering that had been inflicted upon Warhol through the widespread availability and useage of guns in America, it seems natural that he should have represented such objects as cultural icons, which of course they are to a great many Americans. And the personal significance of this imagery is heightened by the fact that Warhol did not just represent any gun here; this is a .32 snub-nosed pistol, of the type that Valerie Solanas had used when attempting to kill him.

The chilling associations of the subject matter are heightened in emotional effect by the fact that the portrayal of each gun is so impersonal. That impersonality accurately mirrors reality of course, for a gun is merely a tool in the hand of the person who wields it, and the visual detachment goes back to the impersonality of much of Warhol's art from the 1960s, where by identical means the painter projected the utter emptiness of modern life, as represented by its artefacts.

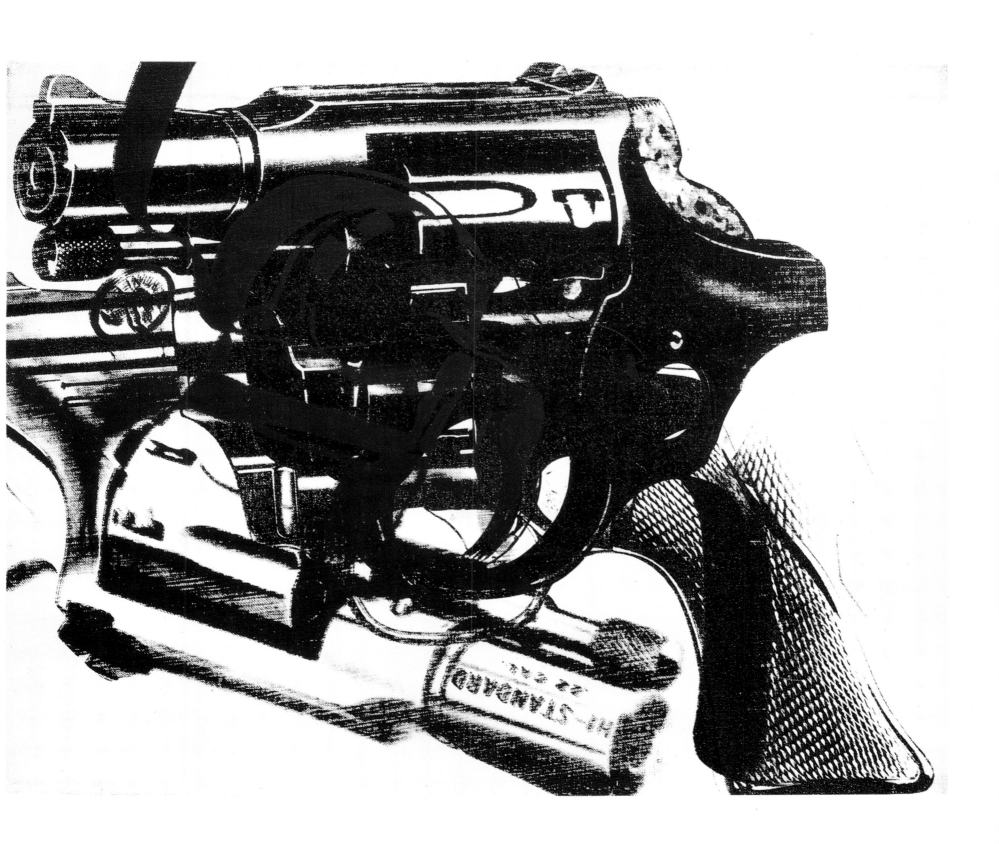

Goethe, 1982

Four screenprints, each 96.5 × 96.5 cm. The Estate of Andy Warhol

Warhol took this image of the great German poet, playwright and philosopher Johann Wolfgang von Goethe directly from the famous portrait entitled *Goethe in the Campagna* by Wilhelm Tischbein (1750–1812) which hangs in the Staedelsches Institut, Frankfurt am Main, Germany, a portrait that was painted when Goethe visited Italy in 1786.

   The *Goethe* series of prints was published in 100 numbered sets of four prints each. Warhol unashamedly created these portraits as a way of appealing directly to the highly profitable German market (for exactly the same reasons a set of Beethoven portraits was created after 1987 by the artist's executors from designs supplied by Warhol). By the addition of 'glamorous' colours, Warhol reminds us that Goethe was a media superstar of the Romantic era, even if the images themselves do not seem to differ very much visually from the types of glamorized portraits that are commonly encountered on the covers of book jackets, record albums and the like.

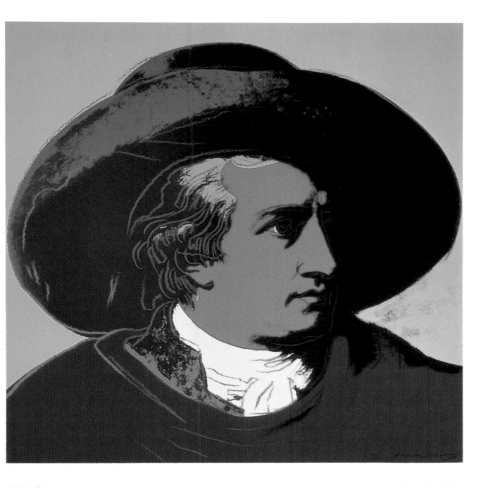
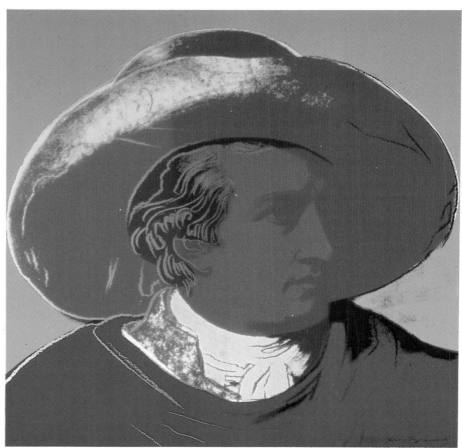
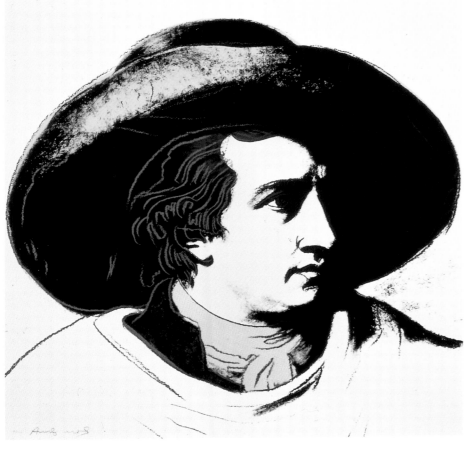
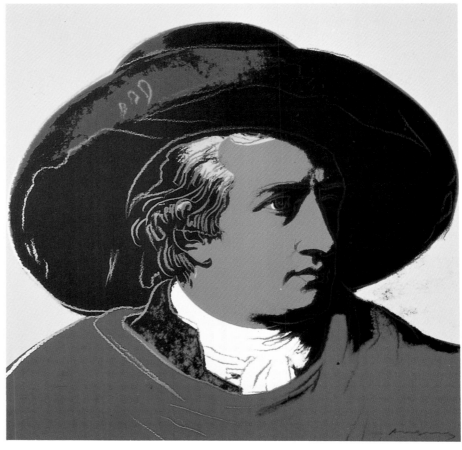

Untitled, 1984 (Painting by Andy Warhol in collaboration with Jean-Michel Basquiat)

Synthetic polymer paint on canvas, 194.3 × 292.1 cm. Private Collection

Warhol's short-lived artistic collaboration with Jean-Michel Basquiat (1960–88) was an unhappy one, as touched upon in the Introduction, and certainly images such as these do not betray his hand at all. Warhol was never at his best when he was using paint expressively anyway, and the intellectual incoherence of the graffiti-inspired imagery of Basquiat was even more antipathetic to his true artistic nature than the subjectivity of this type of painting. The result is a picture that induces the associations of popular culture, but without affording us any purposeful insight into that culture other than the obvious ones that it can look childish and crude.

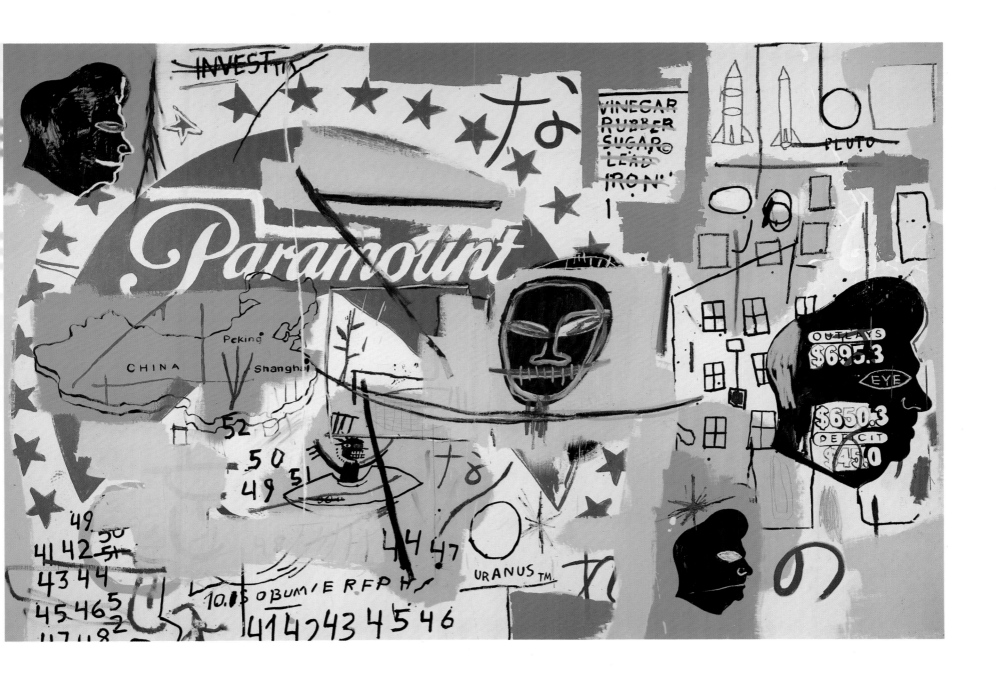

Sixty Last Suppers, 1986

Silkscreen ink over paint on canvas, 294.6 × 998.2 cm. Leo Castelli Gallery, New York

Warhol was invited to rework Leonardo da Vinci's image of the *Last Supper* by his first New York dealer, Alexandre Iolas, who wanted to show the resulting paintings in a gallery that stood opposite the refectory of the Church of Santa Maria delle Grazie in Milan, the building in which Leonardo's original mural is located. However, Warhol did not use reproductions of the Leonardo for his pictures; instead, he employed photographs of two kitsch sculptural reproductions of Leonardo's painting (one in white plastic, the other in Capo-di-Monte bisque), as well as a published line drawing that greatly simplified the Leonardo. Warhol's images are therefore as much a comment upon kitsch or simplified reproductions of religious works of art as they are a rehash of Leonardo's original image.

Warhol explored two approaches in his *Last Supper* pictures. In one he took the line-drawing reproduction of the Leonardo as the starting-point for a series of hand-drawn variations, in several of which the 'cheapo' associations of the imagery were heightened by the addition of numbers that denote the price tags attached to items of quasi-religious junk. In the other approach, Warhol reproduced photographs of the two kitsch sculptures by means of silkscreen printing over paint on canvas, as here. In several of these latter images Warhol coupled his statement about religious art and kitsch with his current interest in camouflage patternings, perhaps to suggest that true religiosity is obscured rather than revealed by such artefacts.

In this work Warhol used the replication of the kitsch Leonardo sculptures to make familiar but still valid points about the replication of both religious icons and religious kitsch, and it matters little whether or not we can see the individual details clearly in reproduction: the repetitiousness of a familiar icon is the point here (and if you want properly to appreciate Leonardo's detailing, then perhaps it is best to visit Milan to look at his original painting).

The opening of Warhol's Last Supper exhibition in Milan in late January 1987, which the artist attended, was his last important public appearance as a media superstar, with over 3,000 people and the mass media mobbing the preview in order to fête him.

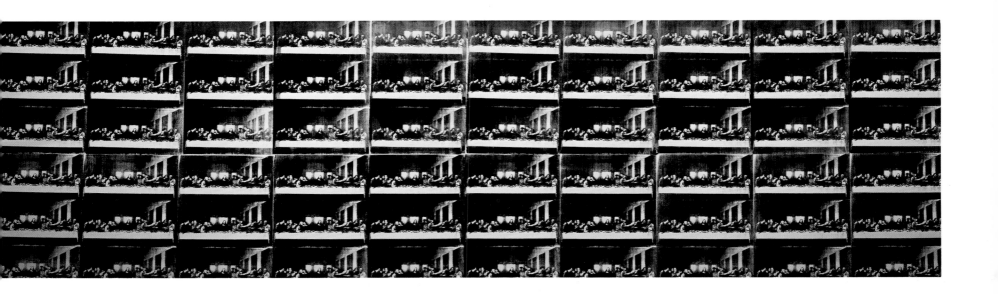

Camouflage Self-Portrait, 1986

Silkscreen ink on synthetic polymer paint on canvas, 208.3 × 208.3 cm. The Metropolitan Museum of Art, New York

The camouflage patternings seen here were derived from some standard United States military camouflage that Warhol had purchased in an army surplus store in 1986. Initially the painter used the camouflage to create a group of abstract paintings, but eventually he put it to much more fruitful employment in conjunction with representational imagery, as in this picture.

After about 1963 Warhol became a master at masking his real self from public gaze. To art critics, art historians and media questioners he usually went out of his way disingenuously to appear naive, mentally slow, emotionally detached and even robotic (for reasons given to Gene Swenson in 1963 that are quoted in the Introduction, p. 18). Yet in private he was very worldly, intellectually quick, frequently emotional, always manipulative (which is a true measure of his worldliness, for manipulativeness necessitates an understanding of human character) and anything but a machine. And intellectually he was highly sophisticated, as his works make abundantly clear. The late series of camouflaged self-portraits therefore projects the real Andy Warhol in a very direct fashion indeed, for camouflage is a means of masking true appearances.

Naturally, the camouflage in these late self-portraits forces the images to the interface with abstraction, that frontier that the painter had explored so often in his earlier works. The spikiness of the hair contrasts strongly with the swirling, curvilinear shapes of the camouflage, and together they imbue the image with a startling visual impact.

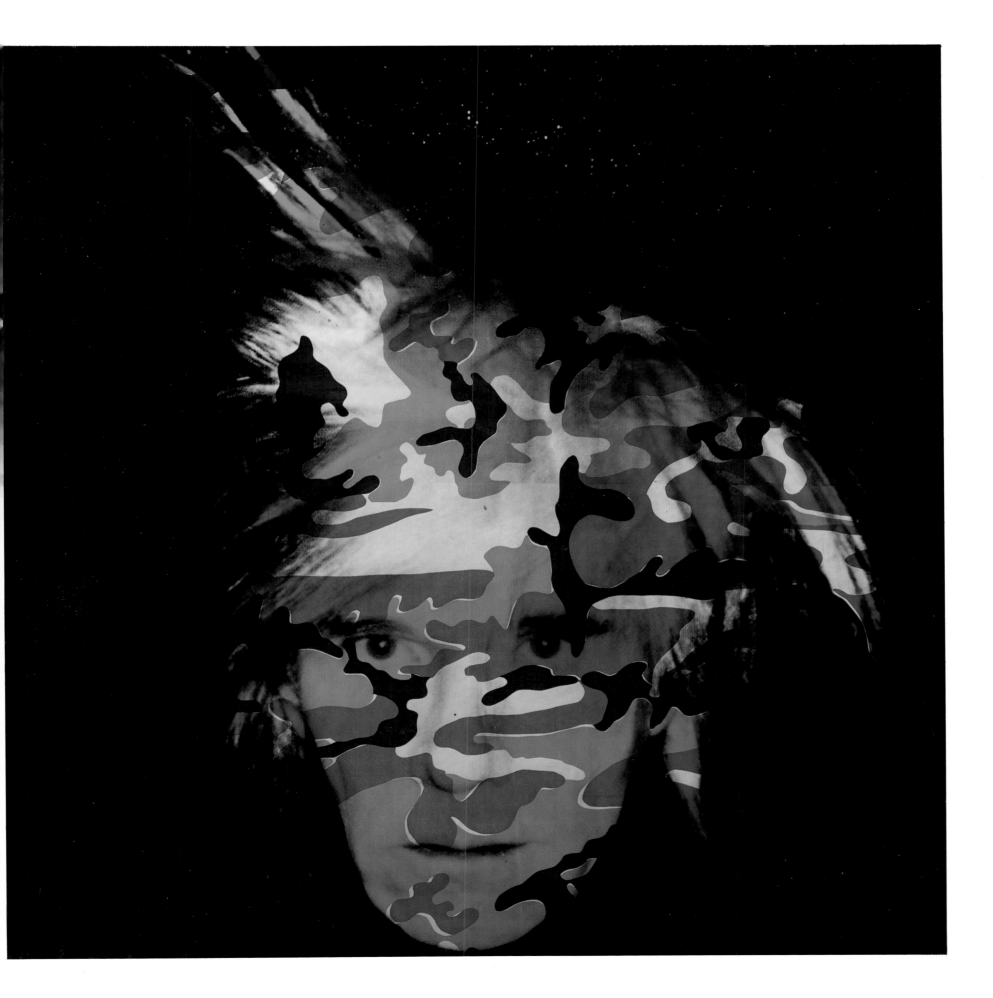

Untitled [Footprints in Sand], 1987

Four stitched gelatin silver photographic prints, overall size 56 × 71 cm. Robert Miller Gallery, New York

Warhol was an avid photographer, and his penultimate exhibition held during his lifetime (and his last show mounted in New York) was of a number of his photographs that had been sewn together in groups of four by Michelle Loud; the exhibition opened at the Robert Miller Gallery in early January 1987 to some critical acclaim and public enthusiasm.

The threads used to join the individual photographs were left hanging over the pictures themselves, as if to remind us that we are looking at artificial constructs, whilst the juxtaposition of the images brings out the inherent rhythms of their internal shapes in ways that would not be nearly so apparent if each image had been viewed separately – once again Warhol was pushing back the frontier between appearances and abstraction, and in the present group of photos perhaps crossing that frontier, for if it were not for the toe-marks on the sand at the bottom right-hand corners of each image, we might well have found it impossible to apprehend exactly what it is in the real world that we are looking at.

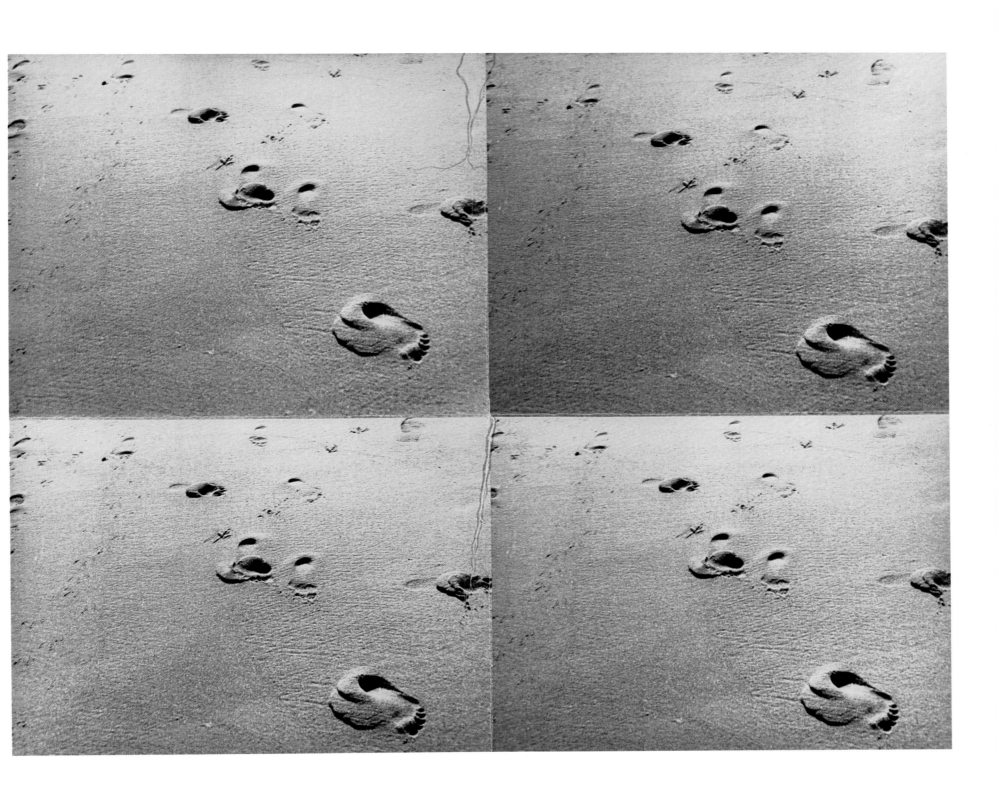

CHRONOLOGY

1928
Born Andrew Warhola 6 August in Pittsburgh, Pennsylvania, the third son of Ondrej and Julia Warhola.

1934
Enters Holmes Elementary School, Pittsburgh.

1936–41
Suffers from rheumatic fever, schooling disrupted.

1941
September, enters Schenley High School, Pittsburgh.

1942
May, father dies from tuberculous peritonitis.

1945
Graduates from Schenley High School. Enters Carnegie Institute of Technology to study art.

1946
Wins the Leisser Prize of $50 for the best summer vacation work made by a student.

1948
Spring, works part-time in the display department of the Joseph Horne department store in Pittsburgh.

1949
March, submits painting entitled *The Broad Gave Me My Face, But I Can Pick My Own Nose* to open exhibition of the Pittsburgh United Artists; jury rejects it. June, graduates with a Bachelor of Fine Arts degree; July, moves to New York with fellow student Philip Pearlstein, with whom he shares an apartment on St Mark's Place, off Avenue A, before moving into a shared apartment on West 21st Street. First illustrations published in leading fashion magazines under the name of Andy Warhol.

1950
March, moves to shared apartment at Manhattan Avenue and 103rd Street. Autumn, moves to own apartment on East 24th Street. Career as commercial artist begins to take off.

1951
Makes first drawings for television, as well as advertisement design that two years later wins him first Art Directors' Club award.

1952
Holds first exhibitions at Hugo Gallery, New York, but sells nothing. Moves to 216 East 75th Street and is joined there by his mother who lives with him henceforth until her death in 1972. With Fred McCarroll and Mary Suzuki illustrates *Amy Vanderbilt's Complete Book of Etiquette*.

1953
Summer, moves to 242 Lexington Avenue. Publishes *A Is an Alphabet* and *Love is a Pink Cake* with Ralph Ward. Wins first Gold Medal of the Art Directors' Club of New York for design made in 1951.

1954
Holds three shows of work at the Loft Gallery on East 45th Street, publishes *Twenty-five Cats Name [sic] Sam and One Blue Pussy*, sells books and drawings through Serendipity shop on 58th Street, active in designing for the *Theater 12* group. Hires first studio assistant, Vito

Giallo, begins relationship with Charles Lisanby.

1955
Obtains commission to make series of weekly shoe advertisement newspaper designs on behalf of fashionable I. Miller shoe store. Autumn, Giallo replaced as studio assistant by Nathan Gluck who works for Warhol until 1964. Publishes *A la Recherche du Shoe Perdu* and exhibits portfolio of *Drawings for a Boy Book*.

1956
February, exhibits at Bodley Gallery but sells only small number of drawings. April, exhibits some drawings in the *Recent Drawings U.S.A.* show at the Museum of Modern Art, New York. June–July, visits the Far East, India and Europe with Charles Lisanby. Receives 35th Annual Art Directors' Club award for Distinctive Merit for I. Miller shoe advertisement. Takes second apartment at 242 Lexington Avenue, begins collecting works of art, including pieces by Picasso, Braque, Klee and Magritte. Publishes *In the Bottom of My Garden*. December, holds successful exhibition of Crazy Golden Slippers drawings at the Bodley Gallery.

1957
January, is featured in two-page spread in *Life* magazine. Wins 36th Annual Art Directors' Club award, as well as Award for Distinctive Merit for I. Miller shoe advertisement. Has operation intended to alter shape of nose. Holds another successful show at the Bodley Gallery and publishes *The Gold Book* as Christmas self-promotional item.

1958
Begins to form idea of becoming fine rather than applied artist after seeing debut exhibitions of Jasper Johns and Robert Rauschenberg.

1959
Buys town-house at 1342 Lexington Avenue between 89th and 90th Streets for $67,000. Loses I. Miller shoe account, although has plenty of other advertising work and receives Certificate of Excellence from American Institute of Graphic Arts for previous year's work. Autumn, publishes joke cookbook, *Wild Raspberries*, with Suzie Frankfurt and holds exhibition of drawings made for the book at Bodley Gallery in December. Is very confused as to sense of direction.

1960
Takes up painting seriously, drawing imagery from advertisements and comic strips, and painting popular culture objects such as Coca-Cola bottles. Work attracts attention of dealer Ivan Karp.

1961
April, exhibits Pop paintings in 57th Street window of Bonwit Teller department store. Begins selling paintings directly to collectors, often at knock-down prices. Los Angeles dealer Irving Blum becomes acquainted with Warhol's work. December, purchases idea for Campbell's Soup-Can and Dollar Bills paintings from gallery owner and interior decorator Muriel Latow.

1962
Makes Campbell's Soup-Cans and Dollar Bills paintings. July, discovers potentialities of silkscreen technique, and also exhibits Soup-Can series of paintings at Irving Blum's Ferus Gallery in Los Angeles. Summer, makes first silkscreen paintings of baseball, movie

and pop music stars, and begins Marilyns series. October, exhibits in group Pop art show at Sidney Janis Gallery. November, makes New York breakthrough with one-man show at influential Stable Gallery. Show is almost a complete sell-out.

1963

May, makes first Race Riot pictures; June, embarks upon first silkscreened Disaster pictures. Rents studio in abandoned firehouse at East 87th Street, employs Gerard Malanga as assistant. Makes first films, including *Sleep*. In autumn drives with friends to Los Angeles for second one-man show at Ferus Gallery. November, moves studio to loft at 231 East 47th Street, henceforth known as 'The Factory'. December, begins Jackie series using photos of Jackie Kennedy at presidential funeral. Begins *Kiss* film.

1964

January, exhibits Disaster paintings at Ileana Sonnabend Gallery in Paris under title of *Death in America*. Makes films, including *Haircut* and *Eat*. Creates 400 wood sculptures of Campbell's Soup Cans, Brillo Pads, Del Monte Peach Halves and similar cardboard grocery boxes which are exhibited at Stable Gallery in April. Also in April exhibits *Thirteen Most Wanted Men* monochrome mural on New York State Pavilion at New York World's Fair; later obliterates image with aluminium paint after political protests. Summer, makes Flower paintings and further films including *Dracula*, *Couch*, *Empire*, *Drunk*, *Hand Job* and *Blow Job*. Has four Marilyn canvases holed in studio by visitor with gun. December, receives sixth annual award of *Film Culture* magazine.

1965

March, involved in Canadian Customs dispute over artistic status of grocery box sculptures. April–May, travels to Paris for opening of Flowers show at Ileana Sonnabend Gallery, thereafter visits London, Madrid and Tangiers with entourage. Creates films, including *Screen Test #1*, *The Life of Juanita Castro*, *Horse*, *Vinyl*, *Kitchen*, *Beauty #2*, *My Hustler*, *Bitch* and *The Death of Lupe Velez*. Summer, begins collaboration with Paul Morrissey. October, holds first solo museum retrospective exhibition at Institute of Contemporary Art, Philadelphia, opening turns into near-riot. December, creates music group Velvet Underground.

1966

April, opens multimedia and music show The Exploding Plastic Inevitable at Polish Cultural Center (the 'Dom') on St Mark's Place, featuring Velvet Underground. Also in April holds exhibition of Cow Wallpaper and helium-filled silver balloons at Leo Castelli Gallery. May, travels to West Coast with Exploding Plastic Inevitable for disastrous music tour. Summer, makes *Chelsea Girls*, his first commercially successful film.

1967

May, visits Cannes for planned film-festival showing of *Chelsea Girls* but film is not shown; later visits Paris and London. Summer, makes further films, *I, a Man* (featuring Valerie Solanas) and *Bikeboy*. Shows six self-portraits in US pavilion at Montreal Expo '67. Autumn, hires impersonator to substitute for him as lecturer at various universities and colleges. Takes on Fred Hughes as business manager.

1968

January, moves studio to new location at 33 Union Square West, also makes film *Lonesome Cowboys* in Arizona. Travels to Stockholm for retrospective exhibition at Moderna Museet. May, makes *Surfing Movie* in La Jolla, California. 3 June, is shot by Valerie Solanas in assassination attempt, and hospitalized until 28 July. Recuperates during remainder of year and paints multiple portrait of Happy Rockefeller in August. Autumn, supervises production of *Flesh* (directed by Paul Morrissey), and produces film *Blue Movie*.

1969

March, has further hospital treatment for gunshot wounds. Visits Los Angeles twice to seek finance for movies but is unsuccessful. Publishes first issue of *Andy Warhol's Interview* magazine in autumn. June, Valerie Solanas receives three-year prison sentence for shooting Warhol and others. 25 June to 5 August, shows homosexual pornographic films in regular cinema to raise money. December, makes most successful film, *Trash*.

1970

May, travels to California for opening of large retrospective exhibition in Pasadena; show later travels to Chicago, Eindhoven (Holland), Paris, London and New York. 13 May, one of Soup Can paintings fetches highest price ever reached at auction to date by living American artist. September, visits Paris to make movie, *L'Amour*.

1971

February, Julia Warhola suffers stroke. Also in February Warhol visits London for opening of four shows of his works; later travels to Cologne and Munich. April, retrospective opens in New York at Whitney Museum of American Art. June, makes film, *Heat*, in Los Angeles with Paul Morrissey. Autumn, Warhol play, *Pork*, is mounted in New York and London.

1972

Winter 1971–2, makes over 2,000 paintings of Chairman Mao, also creates painting and print series of lurid images of Richard Nixon to support presidential campaign of opponent George McGovern. September, flies to Italy for showing of *Heat* at Venice Film Festival. 22 November, mother dies in Pittsburgh aged 80; Warhol does not attend funeral.

1973

Summer, visits Rome to make two movies, *Flesh for Frankenstein* and *Blood for Dracula*. Begins making large numbers of commissioned portraits.

1974

August, moves studio to 860 Broadway. October, visits Paris, Milan and Tokyo. December, receives award from Popular Culture Association for services to understanding of homosexuality.

1975

Begins portfolio of Mick Jagger portrait prints and Ladies and Gentlemen series of prints of drag queens. May, attends dinner held at White House, Washington, to honour visiting Shah of Iran. September, book *The Philosophy of Andy Warhol* is published; undertakes tour of America to promote it, later visits France, Italy and

Britain for same purpose. Moves into new house at 57 East 66th Street, for which pays $310,000.

1976

Spring, makes last movie, *Bad*. With Jamie Wyeth, son of Andrew Wyeth, creates complementary portraits. July, visits Teheran as guest of Shah of Iran. August, makes portrait of Jimmy Carter for cover of *New York Times* magazine, later turns it into print to raise funds for presidential campaign. Begins *Hammer and Sickle* and *Skulls* series of paintings and prints.

1977

May, visits Paris and Brussels for exhibition openings. June, attends reception at White House for artists who had supported Carter presidential campaign. Makes Athletes, Torsos and American Indian series of images, as well as Oxidation series using urine interaction with wet copper paint on canvas. October, visits Paris and Geneva.

1978

Makes Sex Parts pictures, as well as Shadows paintings. Produces own television programme, *Andy Warhol's TV*, on cable television; show broadcasts weekly for about two years but is commercially unsuccessful.

1979

Begins Reversals and Retrospectives series of pictures. May, visits Spain, Monaco, France and England. October, publishes book of photographs, *Exposures*, for which he undertakes US and European promotional tour over next few months. November, Portraits of the Seventies exhibition of portraits held at Whitney Museum, New York.

1980

Makes series of *Portraits of Jews of the Twentieth Century*, as well as portraits of German artist Joseph Beuys. Along with Beuys, Warhol attends opening of shows of the Beuys portraits in Naples, Munich and Geneva. April, publishes book, *POPism*, written with Pat Hackett.

1981

January, attends Reagan inaugural, as well as dinner held to honour Ferdinand and Imelda Marcos. Makes Dollar Signs, Knives, Guns and Myths series of images. Visits Germany, France and Austria. Summer, begins relationship with Jon Gould. October, interviews Nancy Reagan for *Interview* magazine. November, exhibits with LeRoy Neiman at the Institute of Contemporary Art in Los Angeles.

1982

For $2 million purchases new building situated at 32nd–33rd Streets between Madison and Fifth Avenues for use as studio complex; renovation costs further $3 million. Makes German Monuments, Goethe and De Chirico Replicas series. Travels extensively to Europe and visits China.

1983

Travels to Spain and France. Makes poster for Brooklyn Bridge centenary celebration.

1984

Makes Rorschach Test, Edvard Munch and Renaissance Paintings series. Begins artistic collaboration with Jean-Michel Basquiat.

August, starts receiving treatment for stress from chiropractor. October, appears as himself on television programme, *The Love Boat*.

1985

Makes Advertisements series of images, while series of pictures of Queens of England, Denmark, Holland and Swaziland is created entirely by studio assistants following Warhol's instructions. Publishes book, *America*. September, show of paintings made in collaboration with Jean-Michel Basquiat opens at Tony Shafrazi Gallery, by which time neither artist is on speaking terms with the other.

1986

Makes Camouflaged Self-Portraits, as well as Frederick the Great, Lenin, Leonardo *Last Supper*, Cars, Flowers and Campbell's Soup Boxes series of paintings and prints. Also seriously involved in photography. Makes a second series of TV shows, *Andy Warhol Fifteen Minutes*. July, visits London. Is sued for damages by City of Oslo, Norway, for appropriation of Edvard Munch images in paintings. Suffering increasingly from gallstones.

1987

January, exhibition of stitched and sewn photographs opens to excellent reviews in New York. Also in January visits Milan, Italy, for opening of exhibition of *Last Supper* paintings. Makes Rado Watches, Beethoven pictures, begins work on The History of American TV series. 22 February, dies in a New York hospital after routine gall-bladder operation.

PHOTOGRAPH CREDITS

LIST OF PLATES

7: Photo of Andy Warhol in front of his *Self-Portrait*, 1967.

9: *Untitled*, *c.* 1955, watercolour on paper, 57 × 72.5 cm, Private Collection.

12: *A la Recherche du shoe Perdu*, 1955, lithograph watercolour, each 24.5 × 34.5 cm, The Estate of Andy Warhol.

13: *Young man with flower* (from *A Gold Book by Andy Warhol*), 1957, watercolour over print, 35 × 27.5 cm, Private Collection.

14: Jasper Johns: *Flag on Orange Field, II*, 1958, encaustic on canvas, 92.7 × 37.2 cm, Private Collection.

20: *129 Die in Jet (Plane Crash)*, 1962, synthetic polymer paint on canvas, 254 × 183 cm, Museum Ludwig, Cologne.

21: Photo of Andy Warhol with Jasper Johns, *c.* 1964. The Elizabeth Taylor silkscreens are behind them.

23: *Dance Diagram – Tango*, 1962, synthetic polymer paint on canvas, 182.8 × 137.1 cm, Museum of Modern Art, Frankfurt-am-Main, Germany.

25: *Gangster Funeral*, 1963, silkscreen ink on synthetic polymer paint on canvas, 266.7 × 192.1 cm, Dia Art Foundation, New York.

26: Photo of exhibition of *Boxes* at Stable Gallery, 1964.

27: Photo of Warhol's *Flowers* exhibition at the Leo Castelli Gallery, New York, November–December 1964.

29: Photo of exterior of New York State pavilion at New York World's Fair, 1964, showing Warhol's *Thirteen Most Wanted Men* in situ.

31: Photo of installation of *Cow Wallpaper* at Leo Castelli Gallery, New York, April 1966.

35: Still from the film *Trash*, 1970, showing Joe Dallesandro and Holly Woodlawn.

37: Andy Warhol distributing *Interview* magazine on Madison Avenue, New York, November 1983.

42: *Black-and-White Retrospective*, 1979, silkscreen ink on synthetic polymer paint on canvas, 124.4 × 154.9 cm, Galerie Bruno Bischofberger, Zurich.

45: *Peach Halves*, 1960, synthetic polymer paint on canvas, 177.5 × 137.5 cm, Staatsgalerie, Stuttgart, Germany.

47: *Saturday's Popeye*, 1960, synthetic polymer paint on canvas, 108.5 × 98.7 cm, Neue Galerie, Sammlung Ludwig, Aachen.

49: *Before and After 3*, 1962, synthetic polymer paint on canvas, 182.9 × 255.9 cm, Whitney Museum of American Art, New York. Purchase, with funds from Charles Simon.

51: *Do It Yourself (Landscape)*, 1962, synthetic polymer paint and Prestype on canvas, 178 × 137 cm, Museum Ludwig, Cologne.

53: *32 Soup Cans*, 1961–2, synthetic polymer paint on canvas; 32 canvases, each 50.8 × 40.6 cm, Irving Blum, New York.

55: *Baseball*, 1962, silkscreen ink and oil paint on canvas, 232.4 × 208.3 cm, Nelson-Atkins Museum of Art, Kansas City, Missouri.

57: *192 One-Dollar Bills*, 1962, silkscreen ink on canvas, 242 × 189 cm, Marx Collection, on loan to the Städtisches Museum Abteiberg, Monchengladbach, Germany.

59: *Green Coca-Cola Bottles*, 1962, silkscreen ink on synthetic polymer paint on canvas, 211 × 144.8 cm, Whitney Museum of American Art, New York. Purchase, with funds from the Friends of the Whitney Museum of American Art.

61: *Big Torn Campbell's Soup Can*, 1962, silkscreen ink on synthetic polymer paint on canvas, 182.9 × 136 cm, Kunsthaus, Zurich.

63: *Triple Elvis*, 1962, silkscreen ink on aluminium paint on canvas, 208.3 × 152.4 cm, Virginia Museum of Fine Arts, Richmond, Va. Gift of Sydney and Frances Lewis.

65: *Marilyn Diptych*, 1962, silkscreen ink on synthetic polymer paint on two canvases, each 208.3 × 144.8 cm, Tate Gallery, London.

67: *Gold Marilyn*, 1962, silkscreen ink on synthetic polymer paint on canvas, 211.4 × 144.7 cm, Museum of Modern Art, New York. Gift of Philip Johnson.

69: *Marilyn Monroe's Lips*, 1962, silkscreen ink on synthetic polymer paint and pencil on two canvases, 210.2 × 205.1 and 211.8 × 210.8 cm, Hirshhorn Museum and Sculpture Garden, Smithsonian Institution, Washington DC. Gift of Joseph H. Hirshhorn, 1972.

71: *Red Race Riot*, 1963, silkscreen ink on synthetic polymer paint on canvas, 350 × 210 cm, Museum Ludwig, Cologne.

73: *Suicide*, 1963, silkscreen ink on synthetic polymer paint on canvas, 313 × 211 cm, Kunstsammlung Nordrhein-Westfalen, Düsseldorf, Germany.

75: *Tunafish Disaster*, 1963, silkscreen ink on synthetic polymer paint on canvas, 316 × 211 cm, Saatchi Collection, London.

77: *Five Deaths Seventeen Times in Black and White*, 1963, silkscreen ink on synthetic polymer paint on canvas, two canvases, each 262 × 209 cm, Oeffentliche Kunstsammlung, Kunstmuseum, Basel.

79: *Orange Car Crash Ten Times*, 1963, silkscreen ink on synthetic polymer paint on canvas, 269.2 × 208.2 cm, Museum Ludwig, Cologne.

81: *Optical Car Crash*, 1962, silkscreen ink on synthetic polymer paint on canvas, 208 × 208.3 cm, Oeffentliche Kunstsammlung, Kunstmuseum, Basel.

83: *Ethel Scull 36 Times*, 1963, silkscreen ink on synthetic polymer paint on 36 canvases, 202.6 × 363.2 cm overall, Whitney Museum of American Art, New York. Gift of Ethel Redner Skull.

85: *Mona Lisa*, 1963, silkscreen ink on synthetic polymer paint on canvas, 319.4 × 208.6 cm, Blum Helman Gallery, New York.

87: *Blue Electric Chair*, 1963, silkscreen ink on synthetic polymer paint on two canvases, each 266.7 × 203.8 cm, Saatchi Collection, London.

89: *Atomic Bomb*, *c.* 1963, silkscreen ink on synthetic polymer paint on canvas, 264.1 × 204.5 cm, Saatchi Collection, London.

91: *Elvis I and II*, 1964, silkscreen ink on synthetic polymer paint on canvas, two canvases, each 208.3 cm square, Art Gallery of Ontario, Toronto. Gift from the Women's Committee Fund, 1966.

93: *The American Man – Watson Powell*, 1964, silkscreen ink on synthetic polymer paint on canvas, 326.4 × 163.8 cm, American Republic Insurance Company, Des Moines, Iowa, USA.

95: *Most Wanted Men No. 10: Louis Joseph M.*, 1964, silkscreen ink on two canvases, each 122 × 101.5 cm, Städtisches Museum Abteiberg, Mönchengladbach, Germany; and *Most Wanted Men No. 11: John Joseph H.*, silkscreen ink on two canvases, each 122 × 101.5 cm,

Saatchi Collection, London.

97: *Brillo Boxes*, silkscreen ink on synthetic polymer paint on wood, each box 51 cm high × 51 cm wide × 43 cm deep, exhibited at the Stable Gallery, New York, April 1964. The Estate of Andy Warhol.

99: *Flowers*, 1964, silkscreen ink on synthetic polymer paint on canvas, 293.4 × 293.4 cm, The Estate of Andy Warhol.

101: *Jackie*, 1964, silkscreen ink on synthetic polymer paint on 35 canvases, 40.6 × 50.8 cm each, Museum of Modern Art, Frankfurt-am-Main, Germany.

103: *Campbell's Soup Multicoloured*, 1965, silkscreen ink on synthetic polymer paint on canvas, 91.7 × 60.9 cm, Museum of Modern Art, New York. Elizabeth Bliss Parkinson Fund.

105: *Cow Wallpaper*, 1966, silkscreen on wallpaper, 115.5 × 75.5 cm, The Estate of Andy Warhol.

107: *Marilyn*, 1967, nine screenprints on paper from a portfolio of ten, each 91.5 × 91.5 cm, The Estate of Andy Warhol.

109: Colour photo of *Chairman Mao* exhibition at The Leo Castelli Gallery, New York, 1974.

111: *Chairman Mao*, 1972, silkscreen ink on synthetic polymer paint on canvas, 448.3 × 346 cm, Saatchi Collection, London.

113: *Julia Warhola*, 1974, synthetic polymer silkscreened on canvas, 101.5 × 101.5 cm, The Estate of Andy Warhol.

115: *Skull*, 1976, silkscreen ink on synthetic polymer paint on canvas, 38.1 × 48.3 cm, The Estate of Andy Warhol.

117: *Hammer and Sickle*, 1977, watercolour on paper, 71.1 × 102.9 cm, The Estate of Andy Warhol.

119: Colour photo of installation of *Shadows* (1978) at 393 West Broadway, New York, in 1979; silkscreen ink on synthetic polymer paint on canvas, 102 canvases, each 193 × 132.1 cm, Dia Art Foundation, New York.

121: *Truman Capote*, 1979, silkscreen ink on synthetic polymer paint on canvas, The Estate of Andy Warhol.

123: *Eighteen Multi-Colored Marilyns (Reversals Series)*, 1979–86, silkscreen ink on synthetic polymer paint on canvas, 137 × 208 cm, Galerie Bruno Bischofberger, Zurich.

125: *Diamond Dust Joseph Beuys*, 1980, silkscreen ink and synthetic diamond dust on synthetic polymer paint on canvas, 254 × 203.2 cm, Marx Collection, Berlin.

127: *Dollar Signs*, 1981, synthetic polymer paint and silkscreen ink on canvas, 228.6 × 177.8 cm, Leo Castelli Gallery, New York.

129: *Guns*, 1981, silkscreen ink on synthetic polymer paint on canvas, 40.6 × 50.8 cm, The Estate of Andy Warhol.

131: *Goethe*, 1982, four screenprints, each 96.5 × 96.5 cm, The Estate of Andy Warhol.

133: *Untitled*, 1984 (Painting by Andy Warhol in collaboration with Jean-Michel Basquiat), synthetic polymer paint on canvas, 194.3 × 292.1 cm, Private Collection.

135: *Sixty Last Suppers*, 1986, silkscreen ink over paint on canvas, 294.6 × 998.2 cm, Leo Castelli Gallery, New York.

137: *Camouflage Self-Portrait*, 1986, silkscreen ink on synthetic polymer paint on canvas, 208.3 × 208.3 cm, Metropolitan Museum of Art, New York.

139: *Untitled [Footprints in Sand]*, 1987, four stitched gelatin silver photographic prints, overall size 56 × 71 cm, Robert Miller Gallery, New York.

SELECTED BIBLIOGRAPHY

ANTONIO, Emile de and TUCHMAN, Mitch, *Painters Painting*, New York, 1984.

BLINDERMAN, Barry, 'Modern "Myths": An Interview with Andy Warhol', *Arts Magazine*, October 1981.

BOCKRIS, Victor, *Warhol*, New York and London, 1989.

BOURDON, David, *Warhol*, New York, 1989.

—— 'Warhol as Filmmaker', *Art in America*, May 1988.

CROW, Thomas, 'Saturday Disasters: Trace and Reference in Early Warhol', *Art in America*, May 1987.

EXHIBITION CATALOGUE: *Warhol*, Tate Gallery, London, 1971.

FELDMAN, Frayda and SCHELLMANN, Jörg, *Andy Warhol Prints*, New York, 1989.

GARRELS, Gary (editor), *The Work of Andy Warhol*, Seattle, 1989 (collection of essays by Charles F. Stuckey, Nan Rosenthal, Benjamin H.D. Buchloh, Rainer Crone, Trevor Fairbrother and Simon Watney).

GELDZAHLER, Henry, 'Andy Warhol', *Art International*, April 1964.

HUGHES, Robert, 'The Rise of Andy Warhol', in *Art after Modernism: Rethinking Representation*, ed. Brian Wallis, New York and Boston, 1984.

LANCASTER, Mark, 'Andy Warhol Remembered', *The Burlington Magazine*, March 1989.

MCSHINE, Kynaston (editor), *Andy Warhol, A Retrospective*, New York, 1989.

RATCLIFF, Carter, *Warhol*, New York, 1983.

SMITH, Patrick S., *Warhol, Conversations about the Artist*, Ann Arbor and London, 1988.

STUCKEY, Charles F., 'Andy Warhol's Painted Faces', *Art in America*, May 1980.

SWENSON, Gene, 'What is Pop Art?', *Artnews*, November 1963.

WARHOL, Andy, *The Philosophy of Andy Warhol (From A to B and Back Again)*, New York and London, 1975.

—— (with Pat Hackett), *POPism: The Warhol '60s*, New York and London, 1980.

—— (edited by Pat Hackett), *The Andy Warhol Diaries*, New York and London, 1989.